P9-DFV-875

# RAISE THE BAR

# RAISE THE BAR

*An Action-Based Method for Maximum Customer Reactions*

**Jon Taffer**

with Karen Kelly



New Harvest
Houghton Mifflin Harcourt
BOSTON NEW YORK

This edition published by special arrangement with Amazon Publishing



www.hmhbooks.com

*Library of Congress Cataloging-in-Publication Data*
Taffer, Jon.
Raise the bar : an action-based method for maximum customer reactions / Jon Taffer.
pages cm
ISBN 978-0-544-14830-7 (hardback)
1. Management. 2. Customer relations. 3. Success in business.
I. Title.
HD31.T237 2013
658—dc23
2013027145

Printed in the United States of America
DOC 10 9 8 7 6 5 4 3

# Contents

# INTRODUCTION

# Open for Business

No, Sir; there is nothing which has yet been contrived by man, by which so much happiness is produced as by a good tavern or inn.

— SAMUEL JOHNSON,
EIGHTEENTH-CENTURY ENGLISH WRITER

BARS HOLD A DISTINGUISHED place in American history. Settlers colonizing the country understood that establishing a local tavern was of primary importance because it could stand in for absent infrastructure. The second public building built in America was a "public house," or pub. Before the first official government building was opened in 1774, town meetings, legal proceedings, and other public functions took place in taverns and inns. Even as late as 1783, George Washington bid farewell to the officers of the Continental army at the Fraunces Tavern on Pearl Street in New York City. That tavern, established circa 1762, also played a significant role in pre–Revolutionary War planning and continues to welcome customers today. Our independence was first discussed in a bar, as was the Bill of Rights. The American Revolution, the Whiskey Rebellion, and the Stonewall Riots all fermented in bars.

> Along with being a humble and powerful leader, George Washington was also a prominent distiller, operating one of the largest distilleries in eighteenth-century America. A savvy entrepreneur, he made the country's first rye whiskey and sold more than ten thousand gallons each year.

Pubs, bars, and taverns were the centers of our early communities and continue to provide discreet locations where everything from business deals to political candidacies to marriages can be discussed. The sociologist Ray Oldenburg, author of the classic *The Great Good Place,* calls bars a "third place" because, neither home nor work, they serve as a comfortable "other"—an arena that goes to the heart of a community's social vitality by exemplifying a functioning republic. Anyone who frequents bars knows that your title is checked at the door—CEOs, truck drivers, professors, and janitors are social equals within the safe confines of the tavern and often find common ground there. The unique social features of bars make them worthy of study; the organizational microcosm of successful bars teaches us a great deal about effective management and successful entrepreneurship.

I love the bar business for these reasons. Looking back on my career, I realize that I never intentionally chose it; passion drove me toward it. I enjoyed each step I took, so I kept going. My path was anything but direct, however. I started out as a drummer playing with bands on the Los Angeles club circuit in the early 1980s. We played at iconic venues like the Whisky a Go Go, the Roxy, the Troubadour, and the Starwood. (Thirty years later, all but the Starwood are still going strong.)

To make a living while trying to "make my mark" in the music business, I took a job as a doorman at Doug Weston's Troubadour. Since then, I've filled just about every role in the industry: mixologist, kitchen manager, general manager, food and beverage director, VP of operations, and owner. Today I run the largest bar and restaurant trade show in the industry and oversee a whole suite of trade publications as president of the Nightclub and Bar (NCB) media group. But I can't forget the impact the Troub had on my business philosophy and the principles that guide me today. This famous club dates back to 1957 and made worldwide headlines in 1963 when Lenny Bruce was arrested for cursing on its stage. It has launched or helped establish the careers of some of music's most talented performers and bands, including James Taylor, Carole King, Guns N' Roses, Mötley Crüe, and W.A.S.P. In my case, though, the Troub cemented a passion for the bar and nightclub business. My energy, commitment, enthusiasm, and passion for honesty and integrity (as you'll learn in the book) were forged there and helped me succeed as its manager in a surprisingly short time.

From day one on the doorman job, it was very apparent to me that the club had no controls. Employees ate, drank, and gave the profits away by "comping" customers, by giving away food and drinks to their friends, and by over-pouring alcohol without a second thought. This legendary venue was packed every night because of its amazing entertainment — but it never made money.

As manager, I ran the place with cash from a safe, always hoping I would have enough money in there to buy the necessary products and pay the staff. Fixing the Troubadour meant managing people who had never before been supervised or told what to do (and how to do it).

The rock-and-roll work force tested my management chops, but somehow I kept everyone in line and motivated without setting off a mutiny. That was a powerful lesson for me. As a young rookie with no previous training, I learned how to say no, take control, and straighten out a totally disorganized venue. My success at the Troub gave me the confidence to tackle other challenges, accomplish difficult tasks, and meet goals often by sheer will and desire. I have my late mother to thank for the valuable skills that helped me achieve early success. She was a very demanding woman who set very high standards for herself and for me. Without going into too much detail, my relationship with her required that I learn how to understand, predict, and react to her shifting energy and moods accurately in order to get results that were the best for both of us.

I left the Troub to bartend down the street at Barney's Beanery. As a manager at the Troub, I made $250 a week, but as a bartender at Barney's, I could make about $600 a week in those days. It was one of the hottest bartending jobs in the city. So it was a question of income as to why I went from manager to bartender — and honestly, the three bands a night at the Troub were wearing on me. But when Barney's asked me to become a manager again, I made the tough decision to give up that extra income in the short run because I knew that, ultimately, being in management would advance my career in the long run. It's a decision every really good bartender has to make.

Even though Barney's had more "systems" in place than did my previous gig, like better shift scheduling and a well-managed kitchen, it suffered from poorly supervised front-of-house workers. There is no replacement for a fully engaged manager who is present and aware of what's happening on his watch. Within ten minutes of taking my place behind the bar, the lead bartender pulled me aside and said very matter-of-factly, "Jon, we steal here. Each of us takes a hundred dollars a night. So if you don't take your money, the cash registers will be out of whack and the boss will know something's up." I was summarily taught how to cheat the register and use the tip cup as a bank.

This behavior, I knew, wasn't for me. I couldn't treat someone, in this case Barney's owner, with respect while simultaneously stealing from him. The bartender was putting me in a very uncomfortable position, but there was no way I was going to go along with the longstanding "tradition" and look the owner in the eye knowing what was going on behind his back. It wasn't a difficult decision, but I still had a lump in my throat when I sat down with the owner and opened his eyes. As a result of this candid conversation, the old staff was fired, and I was put in charge as head bartender and night manager of Barney's.

Did I feel bad that a thief and his minions had lost their jobs? No — there is never an excuse for theft. We put procedures in place that made stealing cash very difficult. In fact, the owner eventually installed an inventory-management and cost-savings system that audited liquor usage and inventory to increase efficiency and decrease over-pouring. The system was remarkably effective and accurate down to a drop — and impressed me so much that I believe every bar should have such a system.

When you go through an experience like that, you understand how easy it can be for honest people to cave in to peer pressure and become dishonest. How many decent people before me had gone along with the bartender's scam, just to maintain the status quo? It wasn't just the money that was floating out the door — the attitude that ongoing theft created among the workers reduced profits across the board at an otherwise very successful business. None of the employees respected the boss; from front to back, everyone took advantage. That trickled down to customer relations and service. Sure, people kept coming through the doors, but once we got the house in order, eliminated the thieves, and hired people who respected both the boss and the customers, profits increased and guests were better served. We made sure the systems worked well by personally creating reactions in employees that encouraged honesty and ethical behavior. When an employee did something well, he or she was rewarded through recognition, a choice shift, or some other low- or no-cost way that reinforced that preferred conduct. If someone screwed up, we would correct him right away, with respect.

Both bars, as different as they were from each other, taught me that the emotional reactions you have toward a business — whether pleasurable or painful, or as a customer or an employee — are directly related to its potential for success. Every other job I've had since has only confirmed this insight. You cannot have a great business without creating one great, positive reaction after another. When I opened my own bar and hospitality consulting company in 1986, I employed what I eventually called the science of Reaction Management. Without it, I wouldn't be the president of the biggest bar and nightclub show in the world, the number one bar and restaurant consultant in the industry, the producer and host of Spike TV's *Bar Rescue,* or the author of the book you're reading. Managing a business is not rocket science, but it *is* a science — your success lies in the reactions of the people around you.

In *Raise the Bar,* I show you how to put Reaction Management to work in your own business. Notice that certain themes and concepts run throughout the book; operating a business is not done in chunks or within individual pods of isolated management tasks. Creating great reactions in your customers and your employees is an ongoing process, requiring every aspect of the business to work in tandem.

*The* reactions *you create are your most defining moments!*

# 1

# You Sell One Thing: Reactions

People expect a certain reaction from a business, and when you pleasantly exceed those expectations, you've somehow passed an important psychological threshold.

— RICHARD THALHEIMER, FOUNDER, SHARPER IMAGE

MY WIFE, NICOLE, AND I were staying at a big-brand hotel for a couple of days while I was on the road shooting *Bar Rescue.* I'm laughing at myself as I write this, but I did nothing but complain from the moment I arrived. Our room was the size of a postage stamp, while the bed was too high off the ground, all of which left me feeling like an awkward giant. It was obvious that the flaccid bacon on my dinnertime sandwich had been cooked the previous morning. And why were the knife and fork the size of airline flatware? Even though I'm a positive person, it's very easy for little disappointments to bum me out. Nowadays, it's hard not to automatically home in on low hospitality standards. It's frustrating because everything I see is easily preventable. I have to force myself to blow these annoyances off—otherwise, I'd never be able to enjoy a dinner, or just about anything I do in my life.

Admittedly, I am a bit cocky when it comes to guest standards, but not without justification: I have more than thirty-five years of experience working in every aspect of the hospitality business. I *know* that hotels, restaurants, bars, dives, burger joints, and nightclubs are capable of best-of-class excellence. I wasn't always this sensitive — standards didn't make it onto my radar until I was a few years into the business. I'll never forget walking through a major hotel with the vice president of product development for Hyatt International, Frank C. Ansel III. Youthful exuberance made me come off like a big shot even though I was nothing of the sort. We were holding a management and entrepreneurship seminar for the company's East Asia employees. The food and beverage director of the hotel knew we were coming, so he had spruced up the place. Everything at the hotel looked amazing to me, but twenty minutes into the walkthrough, Frank looked at his manager with obvious displeasure. I asked Frank why he was upset.

"You think he's doing things well because you look but you don't see," Frank said. He pulled me over to a table and pointed out that the service plates weren't turned the same way, nor was the flatware placed consistently at each setting. Frank nodded toward a waiter who was pouring out of the side of a pitcher instead of the spout — a real no-no in table service. These are subtle things, but they demonstrated a lack of standards and attention to detail. When "little" things are off, it means more important standards are also probably lacking. That line, "You look but you don't see," has stayed with me ever since. After that day, I have never been able to walk past a dirty carpet or a cracked wall without reacting. I notice everything. Businesses are defined by their details. Now, when I look, I see.

Think about this: Two people get dressed in the morning. One person throws on whatever clothes are available; the other takes the time to select an outfit and make sure it's clean, pressed, and put together. Who makes the better impression? The carefully dressed person is thought of as calmer, more powerful, smarter, and more thoughtful than the sloppy one. In an experiment to test perceptions and appearance, teaching assistants who wore formal clothes were perceived as more intelligent than those who dressed more casually. A Harvard study found that women who wore makeup were considered more competent and likable than their barefaced counterparts. (I love this kind of science because it has practical applications for business owners — that's why I use a lot of it in *Bar Rescue* and in my work as a consultant.)

These lessons are as relevant for businesses as they are for individuals. In a joint study conducted by Cornell and Columbia universities, consumers who encountered either a delay in being seated in a restaurant by a host or a delay in getting a check from their server evaluated *overall* service more negatively than customers who didn't experience those two specific delays. Maybe this seems like a no-brainer to you, but obviously many restaurants don't think enough about it, considering how long it often takes someone to seat you or to bring over the bill once you've requested it.

Think about it. When a customer's expectations for your business don't match reality (e.g., "They are slow when they should be faster, ergo they do not care about me or my time"), his or her perception is affected, oftentimes permanently. Shoddy business presentation and practices affect how much value a customer places on your brand.

In short, your customers notice "off" stuff — don't you? They (justifiably) believe that your less-than-stellar details are "business as usual" and therefore an accurate measure of your entire business.

Generally, though, you won't hear that negative feedback because nine out of ten people who have a negative experience with a business don't mention problems (even on social media); they just never return. Pretty frightening statistic, isn't it? I doubt that's the reaction you're looking for.

So let me try this one out on you. When someone asks what you do for a living, how do you answer? Whatever it is, however you describe it, you've probably got it wrong. That's because you aren't in the service, food, beverage, beauty, law, accounting, merchandising, retail, hospitality, sales, facilities, entertainment — had enough? — fashion, media, education, technology, or whatever other industry you define as your business. I believe you're in the *business of customer and employee reactions.* And I have four rules that govern that belief:

1. Everything we do is part of a process, never a result.
2. Every business process, step, or communication must create a positive customer reaction each and every time.
3. That reaction *is* the product.
4. Any business, no matter what it is, lives or dies by the customer reactions it creates.

My overarching philosophy is this: *all* successful business is about creating the right reactions in customers. The way you present yourself and your business, your curb or Web appeal, your logo, where you put your products or how you place your content, the color of your marketing pieces, price points, dress code — everything you do in your business — creates reactions. The best reactions always make the most money.

I live to create employee and customer reactions. Whether you're in San Francisco, New York, or Exeter, New Hampshire, the product or "vehicle" you use to get a reaction may differ, but the feelings perpetuated by the way you do business are universal.

The theory of reactions is part of cultural anthropology—it's in our DNA. The concept of creating a response is as primal as it gets, a constant that has existed throughout time and across cultures. The leader of an African tribe has the same dynamic set of management skills, confidence, and leadership ability as the head of a corporation in Cleveland. The priest who works hard on his Sunday sermon is not that different from the Saturday night DJ who creates a playlist; after all, they both want to energize and inspire people to keep coming back week after week. Both have to understand pacing: peak too early, people get fatigued and leave; peak too late, people get bored and leave. The delivery of the "message" has to be just right. All thoughtful people achieve their objectives by creating the appropriate reactions.

Likewise, virtually every aspect of your business depends on your customer and staff experience. Everything from the financials to the décor or the look and "vibe" of a bar represents foundations from which you can build an amazing experience-reaction dynamic that translates into money. If any one of these elements steals from a positive customer experience, it robs your business and you of potential (not to mention cash).

As soon as you start to see your business as a reaction-making machine, you begin to make decisions very differently. Think of it this way: A chef isn't preparing an entrée; he is, in fact, preparing a guest reaction. The entrée is the vehicle, not the product. *The product is the customer reaction.* When that plate hits the table, one of two things will happen: (1) the guest *reacts* by sitting up and taking notice, or

(2) the guest does *not* react. If nothing happens, that restaurant or bar is "stuck."

If a restaurant customer doesn't stop talking to her companion and notice the food when it arrives at the table, the establishment is in trouble, or soon will be if the chef doesn't redesign the look of the food on the plate to get a sit-up-and-take-notice customer reaction. I will see that the plate is redesigned five hundred times if necessary—as long as it takes to get it right and get a reaction when it is presented to a guest. Customers either notice you in a positive way or they don't. *And you can control those reactions to a very large degree.* It works whether you're running a storefront operation or a Web-based company, manufacturing widgets or providing a service. In fact, I'm so passionate about this concept, I invented and own the term Reaction Management.

## Your One Must-Have: Positive Reactions

The connection between reactions and revenue is often overlooked by hospitality and management schools. There are five "musts" every business professor teaches: an establishment *must* be convenient, be clean, offer quality service, offer a great value, and be safe. That's all true, but these "musts" are a beginning, not an end point. Achieving them are where customer reactions come in. If all you need are these five basic elements to create a winner, then why do people park ten blocks away from a hot nightclub, step over puddles in its bathroom, squeeze into tiny corner tables, accept rushed service, pay three times more for a drink than the place next door, and walk through a dark parking lot in the middle of the night to get back to their car? How can a spot be so popular if it violates all five "musts"?

A "hit" is transcendent — it offers patrons an experience that produces a powerful, emotionally satisfying reaction. Successful reactions are not about logic; they're about emotions. When you hit a customer's emotions, you reach the Promised Land. That's what this book is about — sound business management may be straightforward and logical, but connecting with people isn't. Don't let the logistics overtake the human touch in your business.

To prove my point, indulge me while I take you on a short trip back in time — to 1983, when hair was big and shoulder pads were broad. I was running a new and now legendary dance club called Pulsations in Glen Mills, a suburb of Philadelphia. The concept for the club was a bigger-than-life, high-tech light and music experience. The excitement started before you even got inside. A large neon sign and mirrored building and doorway were the first indications that you were in for something special. There were weekends when people started lining up in the morning just to be the first inside when the doors opened in the evening. It wasn't unusual for the line to stretch around the building and into our rear parking lot.

Once inside, club-goers experienced heavy-duty sensory overload: we offered eleven different levels, bars that moved around the main room, a well-stocked gift shop, an extensive snack bar, a VIP room, and an Alternative Music Room (the "A" Room). Choreographed dance shows performed by pros were highly anticipated nightly events. Pulsations also had one of the most spectacular lighting and sound systems in the world, designed by Richard Long and Associates (now Gary Stewart Audio), the same designers who worked on the Paradise Garage and Studio 54 in New York City.

The club's main attraction, and the one I am proudest of, was a robot named Pulsar (Pulsar was leased for use in *Rocky IV*). At midnight, this $400,000 technological wonder would descend from the ceiling in a twenty-two-foot spaceship, *Genesis 1,* to flirt and dance with a random female patron. There are only two times I have cried at work, and the first was when I saw Pulsar make his debut on the dance floor of Pulsations. (You can still catch primitive video of Pulsar doing his thing on YouTube; it made an indelible mark on the scores of people who loved the club.) Pulsar reminded me of the reason I got into the hospitality business: to evoke great emotional responses. Making people smile is a pretty cool way to make a living, wouldn't you agree?

Did it matter that people had to stand in line for hours to get in? No. Were there complaints on Sunday Teen Nights about the watered-down sodas? Never. Was anyone concerned that they couldn't hear themselves think let alone have a conversation because the music was so loud? No. Were people disturbed that the main dance floor was packed with twenty-five hundred people and the Alternative Music Room, intended for twenty people at a time, was generally jammed with two hundred — some of them literally bouncing off the upholstered black walls? Not a bit. Could the bathroom floors have been a little cleaner on a busy Saturday night? Probably. Did anyone care that they weren't? Nope.

Pulsations probably broke the five "musts" on a nightly basis. And yet it was the hottest, most talked about club in the Northeast at the time. People would drive three hours from New York City, which had plenty of hot nightclubs in the 1980s, to experience the fun and excitement Pulsations provided. It created in customers some of the most amazing reactions that I have ever been a part of. The club lasted and thrived for fifteen years — longer than Studio 54 or any of its other world-class peers. (When new owners took over, the disco era was ending, and they tried to update the place by bringing in exotic dancers — a tragically misguided effort that failed. We'll talk more about missteps like that in chapter nine.)

Like many businesses, bars and restaurants aren't always logical, but they're always emotional. There is a science to Reaction Management, but you're always appealing to people on a visceral level. Patrons of hot bars are getting something over and above convenience, cleanliness, quality, price, or safety. They're getting something exciting, enthralling, and fun. Of course it all starts with the ambience, the music, the décor, and the look and behavior of the staff — a lot of tangibles that, taken together, create an intangible feeling, the heady heyday of Pulsations being a case in point. The important thing to understand is that if you aren't creating great customer reactions, it doesn't matter how clean and convenient your place is — it's going to be a snore. However, if you don't have those basic five "musts" *and* you're losing revenue, well, you better clean up your act.

## Predict Success

Standards are gold in terms of Reaction Management, so it pisses me off when they're missing. It's like leaving money on the table. My definition of a standard boils down to this: it is qualifiable, quantifiable, and verifiable. If it's not all three, then it's not a standard. You have to know what your purpose and objectives are, and if you're managing others, they need to know the same. What are you doing here and why? I believe the best management fights for standards every day, because if the standards falter, the business falls apart. Small business owners often neglect to identify and maintain standards. It's understandable — you're trying to manage so many different things that formalizing standards seems like a throwaway—but it's not excusable. Establishing standards should be one of the first things you do.

Some of the coolest and most successful bars are the result of management establishing the right standards and then creating systems to make sure they are never compromised. Every night Pulsations followed a precise schedule that was choreographed to the last minute: when the dancers would appear, when live bands would turn the stage over to the DJ, how and when the lighting changed. Every day we had a staff meeting to review the schedule; it was different each night so as not to become predictable to the customers. Nothing happened by chance—every staff member knew what was going to happen when and for how long. We also had standards for appearance (no earrings bigger than a dime on servers, no colored nail polish, and so on), kitchen operations (nothing could take more than twelve minutes to arrive at a table), and beverage service (soft and hard drinks had to be served in appropriate glasses).

There has to be an established process for you to do a walkthrough of your business and determine whether everything is being done right and, if not, how to fix it. What are your markers for the appearance of your building inside and outside, the cleanliness of your bar area and the kitchen, website maintenance, list or database management, bookkeeping, operations, e-mail etiquette, and customer service? What is acceptable and unacceptable to you? At the end of the day when I drive home, I run through all the benchmarks for my businesses in my mind—did I meet my standards? If so, I can get a good night's sleep. If not, I have some work to do. If we all think this way, we will succeed.

When you go to a great restaurant, the details of fine service and presentation are what you remember more than the food: the friendly, welcoming personality of the hostess or maître d', the fresh flower arrangements, the little chocolates delivered on a silver plate at the end of the meal — these small touches can make you feel so good, so important and valued. Same goes for the local diner: the owner who stops by your table to ask after your family, the server who goes the extra mile to make sure your eggs are just the way you like them, the juice that's fresh squeezed instead of poured from a food service can. Makes you feel like someone cares about your experience, doesn't it? Who doesn't want to feel that way? And you want more; you want to go back to get in touch with those wonderful emotions again. What is the equivalent of those details in your business? It's money in your pocket if you pay attention to them.

## Brand Them, Not You

It's not enough to simply "love what you do" and think you can find success by flying by the seat of your pants. I can't tell you how many failed bar and restaurant owners I've met who thought that enjoying bars or being a "foodie" qualified them to run a successful establishment. They create places as monuments to themselves, with never a thought to the customer. It makes me laugh when the same people talk about "branding" as if a brand based on an interior monologue will automatically elicit a positive response from customers. Your "brand" is what your customers think of you, not what you think of you.

When an inevitable obstacle or problem appears — personal or professional — these are the owners who tune out or blame the customer, the economy, the bad location, or just about anything but themselves. It doesn't take long for them to come to hate the sight of a martini glass or a pile or potatoes. I always ask these people: What the heck did you think you were doing?

During season one of *Bar Rescue,* we met Domenic Centofanti, who had bought the historic Downey's Restaurant, an Irish pub in Philadelphia. An unrealistic belief in the power of the Downey's name and his own reputation as a respected chef had brought him to the brink of bankruptcy. Domenic may have been well known among city diners, but he had never been an owner/manager and had no experience running anything outside of a kitchen. Management was broken because the bar lacked standards. There were no operational manuals, and the staff had never been taught procedures. No one was in charge — least of all Domenic. When things started going south — low head counts, lackluster service, complaints about the food, poor property maintenance — he blamed customers for his business failings.

"Failings" is an understatement. At one time, Downey's made about $2 million a year — hauling in $40,000 a week on food alone. After Domenic took over, yearly revenues fell by more than half. Downey's had no standards in place that reinforced its Irish pub "feel" or authenticity. It offered only four Irish whiskeys of the multitude on the market that could have been available. Domenic had also reverted to his comfort zone by adding a page of Italian dishes to the menu, which was just plain weird. Pasta is not something visitors to an Irish pub expect or really even want. Moreover, they aren't going to instinctually trust the quality and taste of Italian pasta dishes offered in an Irish restaurant.

What kind of Reaction Management was necessary to revamp and reinvigorate Downey's — and make it as profitable as I knew it could be? What did we need to do to get more people into Downey's and get them to spend more money, stay longer, smile more, interact with one another, and have a better time? The staff had to relearn service procedures, and Chef Domenic had to take the helm as manager. The menu had to be simplified and it had to feature appropriate Irish-centric beverages and food. The historic pub feel had to be prominent, and we had to inject the feelings of fun and friendship people expect from an Irish bar. Working with rock-star Irish chef Brian Duffy, we made the menu authentic again by adding dishes like shepherd's pie, corned beef and cabbage, bangers and mash, and fish and chips. Whiskey expert and Philadelphian Keith Raimondi taught the bartenders about Irish whiskey and incorporated several interesting brands into the bar menu. When we reopened the pub, guest reactions were very different. One month later, we looked in on Downey's and revenues were up by 15 percent.

None of the changes we made, by the way, were particularly expensive. The makeover didn't require a major construction renovation — we kept a lot of the pub's original and charming features, like the well-worn wooden floor and the island bar. We only installed a new stove since the old one had literally fallen apart, making it a necessary capital expenditure.

That's the thing about creating customer reactions — it doesn't mean spending big bucks. A lot of it comes down to common sense, an understanding of the psychology of consumer behavior, and a respectful awareness of your audience and environment.

As we did with Downey's and all the businesses we work with, you have to consciously ask yourself: What do my customers want and expect, and what kinds of reactions do I want them to have? Put the answers down on a piece of paper so you can see them in front of you — they're easier to work on when you declare them in writing.

You really have to be that direct and elementary as you shift your business philosophy to Reaction Management.

There's a caveat to everything I've just said, of course. You need to understand that it's twice as hard to run your own show. If you think the pressure of being a boss in a company is relentless, the pressure as an owner and entrepreneur and the financial worries that go with it are far more difficult than being an executive in a large organization. The decision to become an entrepreneur is almost irrational. What's the motivation — freedom? Right. Running a business is one of the most demanding jobs in terms of time that I know of. It also means you have to believe that what you're doing or about to do doesn't exist in quite the way you can do it, that you're filling a hole and satisfying an unmet need.

Besides, getting people to part with their hard-earned money is tricky in this economy, no matter what kind of business you're in. None of us can afford to wait for the current environment to change. We have to adapt or die. It's time to change the way you view your business by remembering you are in the business of creating customer reactions — period! If you stick with me on this premise, I promise that you will:

- **Connect with** your audience
- **Gain** a competitive advantage
- **Bring in** more customers than ever before
- **Significantly increase** customer spending
- **Prompt** strong word of mouth and **generate** many more referrals

- **Increase** revenue
- **Build** powerful brand loyalty and brand equity

If you can cultivate a consistent desire within yourself to engage your customer by generating reactions, you will be successful. That desire is what I hope to inspire in you — so get on my bus. I'm ready to leave and I don't want you to miss the journey.

# 2

# You as a Reaction Manipulator

What's measured improves.

— PETER F. DRUCKER, MANAGEMENT CONSULTANT

ANGELS SPORTS BAR sat on a ribbon of blacktop on the edge of Corona, California, a middle- and working-class town nestled against the Santa Ana Mountains about forty-eight miles from Los Angeles. Owner Renee Vicary could have stepped right out of a film noir—busty, blond, and tattooed, her handsome face perpetually swollen from exhaustion.

When my wife, Nicole, and I paid an anonymous visit to Angels, we were turned off from the get-go. If I can't personally visit a bar before trying my best to save it on my show, I often enlist my wife or daughter or hospitality pros I know to do some reconnaissance so we know firsthand what's not working. It's always eye-opening. Then we can talk to the owner honestly, devise a management plan and a makeover, and then implement the changes.

In Angel's case, it wasn't that our waitress was unfriendly; she was nice enough, if somewhat inattentive. It was her skanky outfit and overly casual service that really turned us off. She served us a pizza that was still sitting on the cardboard food-service tray it came in—sure, you can blame the kitchen for that, but the waitress could have done something about it too, like taking three seconds to transfer the pizza to an actual plate. And the fact that we didn't touch the food didn't even register with her—or maybe it did, but she simply didn't care enough to ask if there was a problem with our meal. Meanwhile, the credit card machine was "broken," conveniently enough, so she pointed us to an expensive ATM machine in a dark corner. (Exorbitant ATM fees bring extra revenue into bars; taking charge cards costs bars and other businesses money.)

Angels' service wasn't always this dismal. There was a time when it was one of the most popular sports bars in town, raking in between $85,000 and $90,000 a month. Now, however, Renee was in desperate straits: losing $4,000 a month, she spent most of her time sitting in the back office staring at bills she couldn't pay. It's unclear when the cycle of losses and disregard for managing began, but it was clear when I arrived that Renee's distant and disinterested behavior was firmly entrenched and had created a series of destructive reactions in her employees and her customers. This had bred lousy attitudes among the staff and attracted a glut of undesirable customers who discouraged other, potentially paying patrons from setting foot in the place.

One of the ingredients for a successful bar is a sense of playfulness or fun. As sociologist Ray Oldenburg explained to me, "One of the indicators of this is laughter." In his book *The Great Good Place,* Oldenburg cited a study he conducted where he assigned some of his students to measure laughter in bars. The average American laughs seventeen times a day, and Oldenburg's students found that the frequency of laughter in successful bars was many times that number.

"There is a lot of teasing and camaraderie, along with the welcoming of newcomers [in successful bars]," Oldenburg observed. There was no playfulness or laughter at Angels, however, and newcomers who weren't sent packing by the lousy service were often stared down by other patrons and eventually made to feel uncomfortable.

In my thirty-five years as a hospitality consultant, I hadn't come across a bar quite as pathetic as this fallen angel. Cleaning up and redesigning the place was important, but compared to helping Renee create the right reactions in her employees, the physical revamp would be a piece of cake. Now, I rarely have time for subtlety when I'm filming *Bar Rescue* because we have only a few days on each location. Moreover, I knew that Renee's hot button was pride; I could manage her reaction by needling her on that point. I had noticed that her office was the only part of the bar that was organized and clean. Her nails were also perfectly manicured. It was very easy to home in on exactly what I needed to say to get her attention: "Your bar is a shithole," I told her. "You're failing because of the decisions you're making."

Renee desperately wanted the bar to succeed, but she was suffering from management paralysis. It didn't take her long to drop the tough exterior and reveal her fears to me as we did a walkthrough of the space. She soon couldn't hold back her tears.

"I don't want to close," she told me with a tremble in her voice. "I love this place."

Good. That showed me a glimmer of hope. An emotion that triggers a bout of sobbing is one I can build on because it demonstrates that the owner cares.

The next day Renee gathered the staff for a meeting.

"You'll be working for me for the next five days," I told them, "so you either get on my bus or I'll run you over." A little more Reaction Management of my own — these people were so used to ignoring the weak commands of ineffectual management that I knew they weren't going to pay attention to anyone who wasn't direct, tough, and specific. I asked for the head manager, and a fellow named Wayne took the credit. "Congratulations, Wayne, this is one of the worst operations I've ever seen." His duties, he explained, were limited to playing pool with the regulars, drinking, and occasionally fixing a broken outlet "so no one gets electrocuted." He admitted he didn't care, "because Renee doesn't care." Where was Renee while Wayne was doing his thing? Normally, hibernating in the back office.

No wonder this place was bleeding money.

Every failing business has an owner who first failed *as an individual* to achieve the right reactions in customers and employees. I can't change what they've done in the past, but I can show them another way of thinking and acting and hope they'll take my advice and change their behavior. Motivated people do begin to deliberate — quickly — before they speak or act. The process of teaching self-awareness is not always pretty because it demands personal accountability. It can get very ugly before a person agrees to get excuses off the table and go to work, especially among failing bar owners who tend toward denial and blaming circumstances "beyond their control." Frankly, it doesn't always work — the rescued bars that don't make it end up closing because the owners just cannot change their ways. It is extremely difficult to change a person's behavior in the short time we are there. But I thought Renee had potential because she was a fighter.

I convinced Renee that she needed to be fully present, emotionally and physically, in the front of the house, instead of spending hours in her office paying bills (or pretending to). Bookkeeping and administrative duties could be done during the day, when customer traffic was lightest. Or an outside independent contractor could maintain the books — not a terribly expensive service and one that, in the long run, can actually save the owner money by freeing her to focus on Reaction Management. One way or the other, Renee needed to spend more time checking on staff and customers, asking them sincerely how they were doing, as well as making sure the bathrooms were clean and that the glasses behind the bar were being properly washed and dried throughout the night.

Employees and customers alike noticed when Renee became more involved and conscientious. The regular patrons, mostly bikers, started acting more like gentlemen. "Patrons aren't throwing their napkins on the floor anymore," Renee observed after the turnaround was completed. "I'm different and the atmosphere is different, so the guys act differently."

Renee approved of the new sexy yet respectable T-shirts we supplied the staff, and she demonstrated her wealth of knowledge about service standards when we trained the staff to pour properly and observe basic rules of etiquette when handling customer orders. Renee knew what was wrong — but until *Bar Rescue* came in she hadn't been motivated to do anything about it. Failure had put her into a funk.

Most of the employees reacted to the training by rising to the occasion. The now well-trained staff looked more presentable than before and behaved in a more civilized and enthusiastic fashion — in great part because Renee changed the way she behaved toward them. She treated the mainly female staff like respectable, competent professional bartenders and servers, and they reciprocated by acting in a proficient manner. The exception was Wayne. No matter what we tried to do to change his perspective, and no matter how hard Renee tried to show him respect, Wayne refused to improve his attitude or work habits. So we fired him.

You get what you give. Renee accepted what was wrong and had confidence to follow through. She was willing to practice Reaction Management. At the time, I didn't know that my help might have come too late. Months after leaving Renee in what I thought was good shape, her story took a turn for the worse. (As they say, a fish stinks from the head.) In the summer of 2012, Renee had some problems with the law arising from her business. As of this writing, I don't know whether Renee is guilty. If she is, her problems may have started when the business first got into financial trouble — bad management can spiral out of control, leading to a level of desperation that can tempt those who aren't fully committed to ethical standards. You have to be a reasonable person with integrity or there is no future for you: no more positive transactions, no more reactions to be profitably managed.

## Reactions Begin and End with You

Renee's reported legal troubles demonstrate just how much pressure managers and owners are under in today's business world. Sometimes problems arise because of circumstances beyond our control; other times, we make them worse when we allow small issues to multiply and metastasize. However, you *can* control the reactions of other people, and how you personally choose to do this affects your success. You are or should be the best advertisement for whatever business you're in. *You* are the first link in the chain of reactions your business creates — and in large part your personal behavior defines how employees and customers respond to you and whatever you are selling.

Say hello with a smile to a customer and you make a positive difference in his attitude toward what you're selling. Scowl at that same person or keep him waiting for twenty minutes and that'll cause a reaction too, and it won't be pretty. One reaction will lead to a sale, now or in the future, and the other will lead to the loss of a sale and repeat business. Other reactions follow — the patron who gets a smile will think and speak of you kindly; the other patron will do the opposite. And the chain continues from there. Great operators and managers make connections, one person at a time. It's up to you to decide what kind of reactions you want. Once you do that, it's not difficult to shape your actions to accomplish the results you're after.

To be a successful catalyst, you have to love looking people in the eye every day. That requires "front-to-back" thinking. By that I mean you start thinking about your business right at the door, or behind the counter, and move back from there to the service centers, bar, kitchen, storage, back office, and loading dock — exactly the advice I gave Renee. It is very easy to get detached from your business by avoiding its public spaces. I have to look customers in the face each day; I have to see their body language and the flow of things. It haunts me if I don't see these things. I deal with hundreds of people. At one point I had a thousand employees and I was lucky to get twenty seconds with each of them over the course of a year, so those interactions had to count for both of us. Without "front-to-back" thinking, I wouldn't be at the top of my field, the best hospitality consultant in the business.

Our personal power to control reactions and outcomes is exactly why we should start thinking of ourselves as catalysts for positive reactions. When you consciously and deliberately influence reactions via your own behavior, every interaction ends up where you need it to be—with the other party wanting more. To get more of the reactions they enjoy, your employees will stick around, stay on board, and continue to be honest and loyal.

Here's my final wisdom on what makes a business sing. I learned about Reaction Management as a kid growing up in a tough household—but I certainly wasn't thinking about the process in business terms until I was in my twenties. Growing up, thinking and acting in terms of other people's reactions was just about getting through the day with some peace. When I was about twenty-four and starting my career in the hospitality industry, I put the pieces together about what managing the reactions of others could mean to me professionally. When I started consciously putting Reaction Management into practice, I got promoted eleven times in five years and increased my income 800 percent, believe it or a not, before starting my own company. When people react to me in a positive way, I get better jobs, make more money, and take my pick of plum projects. When my employees react well to me, I create teams of people who fight for my business and for me, and who do great work every day.

## Bad Reactions Cost Money

The hospitality industry is one of the largest people-oriented businesses, so your skills as a reaction manager play a vital role in your ability to generate revenue. People take how they are treated in hospitality venues more personally than just about anywhere. Creating bad reactions through "negative manipulation" is costly, as evidenced by the money pit Angels had become. I know this from years of experience, of course, but researchers at the University of Southern California and Georgetown University have quantified it.

In a study, researchers found that uncivil outbursts, as well as other kinds of rude behavior directed at customers (as well as fellow employees), were witnessed, astonishingly, *once a month* in hospitality venues by approximately one-third of the customers they studied. The thing is, customers rarely point out bad experiences to managers or owners, and this creates a perpetual cycle of bad behavior in employees, depressed customer loyalty, and diminished sales and profits. In Renee's case, it also created unruliness and disrespect among patrons.

The study also found that witnessing an employee act in an uncivil manner made customers angry, creating a desire to "get back" at the business by going elsewhere in the future and discouraging others from doing business there as well. "Regardless of the perpetrator or the reason, witnessing incivility scalds customer relationships and depletes the bottom line," wrote the study's authors.

Managers could further exacerbate the situation by reacting to a complaint by harshly scolding the employee in front of the customer. This only makes things worse. Bad management has a trickle-down effect — if you're acting like a jerk in reaction to employee insubordination, there's a good chance you caused it in the first place.

You're still leading by example when you act badly. The employee won't be motivated to deliver results for someone who just humiliated him publicly. Who is the idiot in this situation? Perhaps this was a really good employee who had a lapse. Isn't it better to remain calm, model the preferred behavior to both customer and employee, and reprimand the employee privately?

In fact, the best response in acute circumstances like this is a simple, polite, and calm apology, which researchers said customers perceived as "just and proper" and went a long way toward repairing what was a failed interpersonal business transaction. However, the most effective approach in the long run is developing training programs that foster civility and teach employees to behave the way you want them to behave . . . we're back to standards, aren't we? Together, training and modeling friendly, professional conduct yourself will prevent harmful outbursts and encourage behavior that promotes positive reactions in customers.

Now, those of you who watch *Bar Rescue* regularly are probably thinking, "Um, Jon, you're always yelling at the employees in front of customers." Guilty as charged. Filming the show, I have just days to wake people up, so in those circumstances, I'm more prone to using Gestalt psychology than the Management 101 practice of "praise in public, criticize in private." Diplomacy has to be sacrificed when the clock is ticking and the team is so far down the hole that the only resort is a loud wake-up call. In situations like this, fury is the reaction I want — I get them angry on purpose. This gets them to a place where they will tell me how they really feel. Once I know that, we can start to make improvements.

I have to see if these people care. And I know from experience how to express anger, how to look at someone and say, "Fuck you, you're an asshole," and thirty seconds later reel him back in and create some warmth between us. Regardless of how it looks on TV, I never explode unintentionally or because I have genuinely lost my temper — I never lose my temper. Everything I do on the show is deliberate. Keep in mind, expressing anger in a way that will be constructive is very difficult. Unless you know how to reel a person back in, I do not recommend using anger as a tool in Reaction Management. Stick to what the professors tell you and be honest but calm.

## We're Wired for Reaction Management

I'm skilled at managing people's reactions and have been my whole life; as a result people like my leadership style and would almost follow me off a cliff. I read how people feel and adjust my own approach to get them where I need them to be. I know when I'm losing someone and how to pull him back in. I have managed to "spec" behavior, or change my approach to someone based on subtle feedback he is sending, and stay a step ahead by developing sensitivity to other people's feelings. At Downey's back in chapter one, I had to pull Domenic out of his funk. But he was a complex character with problems that went beyond the bar, including his brother dying in tragic circumstances. I fluctuated between expressing physical warmth by touching Domenic's arm or putting my arm around his shoulders, and yelling at him while poking my finger into the DOMENIC embroidered on his chef's coat. Whatever emotion I needed to tap into determined the strategy I'd use. When people are emotional they become less detached and more real; I can work with real.

If this sounds manipulative, you're exactly right. There's nothing wrong with using manipulation to help your business. Manipulation's thoughtful use is required in life and work, and it's a natural part of human nature. Cultural anthropologists have long understood that interpersonal Reaction Management is present in every culture. Experts often describe the phenomenon as one-to-one reciprocity (our natural instinct to give and take our fair share), which can be exploited through what we call manipulation to strengthen social and business transactions.

In other words, our sense of reciprocity and our desire to influence the reactions of others is hardwired into our brains, making it as primal a behavior as it gets. We cry as infants to get our needs met: food, comfort, a clean diaper. Once we learn how effective a piercing wail can be — the breast arrives, the cuddle is offered, the bottom is cleaned — we begin to refine our Reaction Management skills. Ideally, our "manipulation" of others should be compassionate and mutually beneficial, but it can and does have a dark side, obviously.

Research by the renowned neurologist Antonio Damasio shows that our emotions are enmeshed in the neural networks of reason and logic. In other words, there is no such thing as a decision free of emotion, even though we often hear the idea that making decisions "unemotionally" is a virtuous goal to be aspired to. It's impossible. Customers don't make buying decisions logically, relying solely on "objective" factors such as price, features, or functionality. They use their emotions to make decisions even when they believe they are making cold and calculated ones. The emotional component of decision making is one you can and should play on.

One encounter that brought this home to me was with Jonathan Dolgen, the former chairman and CEO of the Viacom Entertainment Group, a unit of Viacom. My meeting with Dolgen centered on my efforts to secure the go-ahead and financial backing to create a destination restaurant based on its successful TV Land channel. It called for eighty different television series spanning decades to be under one license — a seemingly insurmountable task that had never been done before in Hollywood. I had every TV Land show on board, meaning the restaurants could feature scenes and memorabilia from favorites including *Cheers, Taxi, Hogan's Heroes, I Love Lucy, The Dick Van Dyke Show, Frasier, The Brady Bunch,* and many others.

It had taken me two years of working my way through other, junior executives to get to Dolgen, the man who ran the show, the God of the studio lot, the ultimate decision-maker. Now all the time and money came down to this one meeting.

I'd come fully prepared, with amazing visuals and compelling demographic information. But Dolgen had a reputation—he'd been described as having the "big-browed omnipresence of a gargoyle" and was known as a "bloodletter" not afraid to slash budgets and question costs vociferously. He was also known as a master manipulator. He reportedly had his assistant ramp up the air-conditioning in rooms where he planned to negotiate contracts and other deals. He would then arrive at least thirty minutes late, leaving his opponent waiting in a freezing cold room. By the time Dolgen arrived, he would already have the upper hand, as the other person was stressed out, irritated, and shivering. To top it all off, Dolgen was known as a yeller. Had I met my match?

A cloud of smoke greeted me as I entered Dolgen's office. We shook hands and Dolgen immediately blew more smoke in my face, another quirk he was famous for. He sat down on his office sofa, looked at me, and said, "So you want to be a director?"

"I've been an entertainment director for a long time. I think you'll benefit from my experience." I figured it was best to play it straight and be polite, and to stare directly into his eyes in a positive, nonthreatening way that would force a connection.

Dolgen told me I had twenty minutes to make my case. I put the three-foot-wide creative boards on the chair next to me so I could explain the concept of the restaurant to him, and the damn things kept sliding off the chair.

He then stood, picked up a leather beanbag from his desk, and tossed it to me.

"Try this," he said, gesturing to the falling displays. The weight worked, and I gave him my spiel. It became obvious that Dolgen was getting more and more interested. For more than ninety minutes he asked me a string of questions and threw out ideas of his own. When we were done talking, we stood up and shook hands. I handed him back his beanbag.

As we were walking toward the office door, he put one hand on my shoulder and, with the other, dropped the beanbag in my jacket pocket.

"You might need this again," he said. When I felt the weight of it hit my pocket, I knew I had my deal with Viacom, and confirmation came the next day. Meanwhile, Jack Lemmon was waiting outside to take the next meeting — the whole scenario was surreal. Without successfully reading Dolgen's mood, I wouldn't have lasted twenty minutes, let alone ninety, nor closed the deal. Since I did, I knew I could get through to him by displaying unwavering confidence.

Once you identify the emotional signature associated with a reaction, you can feel and feed that emotion with empathy. You want to do things that you know will make the customer or the other person involved in a business transaction feel comfortable, respected, and valued. When you do this, the positive energy of your emotion moves very quickly between you and the other person. Fear, annoyance, or any of the other more troublesome emotions you might simultaneously be experiencing won't hijack the good feelings. In

Dolgen's case, the emotions he was sending me were hard-assed and all business. I rose to the occasion by becoming a hard-ass too and throwing it right back at him. In response he treated me like a colleague and a gentleman — and we had a deal. In a moment like that I followed his lead. So go ahead and let the other person define the playing field, and then win on that field.

## You Can Be a Master Manipulator

Anyone can learn how to manipulate reactions in others for mutual benefit, mainly because there is a sameness to manipulation. It is predictable, once you understand the basic ways people respond to a stimulus. Here's an experiment: Shake your head yes while someone is talking to you and see if they start shaking their head with you. If they do, you've just manipulated them into agreeing with you.

The first mistake many people make in Reaction Management is not having integrity — remember Renee's legal problems? If an employee or a customer does not believe my intentions are good, then I have no chance of successfully managing his or her reactions and behavior. If you do not build a reputation for making things right, eventually you won't be able to manipulate anyone.

Let's say you go to a restaurant and there is something wrong with the food. If the manager deals with it in a lackluster way, there's a good chance you will never return to the place. But if he comes over to you with sincerity and expresses how awful he feels about what happened, you will sense his desire to build a relationship with you. If he is really good, he'll say, "I want you to come back next week, and I want to sit down with you afterward to see what you think." Better yet, he'll hand you a coupon for a free meal or a round of drinks. This person has just taken a negative situation and pulled you back from it. That's what winners do.

The legendary grocery entrepreneur Stew Leonard Jr. told me a simple but instructive story. The store had run a chopped meat special for a week, and just one day after it had ended, an elderly woman brought some chopped meat to the cash register expecting it to be rung up at the sale price. The customer made some noise when her expectations about price weren't reflected at the cash register. The well-trained checker called Stew Jr. over to assess the situation.

"I didn't like the look on the customer's face," he told me. "She was obviously not just disappointed but angry." Even though he could have made the legitimate argument that the sale was over, he gave her the sale price and in doing so changed the emotional dynamics of the situation. There's no profit in upsetting a regular customer and letting her leave with a bad taste in her mouth. "It would cost far more if this small issue was not made right," he explained.

Extending the sale date for this one customer didn't really cost a thing. But doing otherwise would have left a lingering bad feeling in the customer, which would have ramifications if practiced on a consistent basis. Wouldn't you rather be known as a magnanimous shopkeeper than a rotten, cheap bastard who can't even give an old lady a break? Do whatever is necessary to promote your fairness, because the reactions that come from that offer many rewards.

We tend to avoid uncomfortable situations, and this tendency makes it impossible to effectively manage reactions in others. Never leave unfinished business or unacknowledged emotions on the table. If you leave something dangling — a fear or concern around unfairness or mistreatment — the relationship becomes like a biscuit dropped in a glass of water: it falls apart and eventually disintegrates.

No matter how much you dislike someone, if he or she can offer you a benefit in a current or future transaction, always make what's wrong right. One of my most memorable examples of manipulating a situation for a desired outcome was at Barney's Beanery, the early management position I mentioned in the introduction. It proves that you don't have to travel deep into remote villages in far-off lands to see the anthropology of reciprocity in action.

Barney's was a scene that attracted, as it does now, a Hollywood crowd that ranged from celebrities to crew members to writers to extras — everyone. One late afternoon, not long before happy hour, a group of rough bikers walked in wearing gang colors, ordered pitchers of beer, and took over a table in the restaurant area. This was before motorcycle riding became the province of middle-aged men trying to reclaim their youth. At any rate, the owner didn't want them in the restaurant area if they were just planning on drinking. There was a posted rule in the establishment: the bar was for drinking, and the restaurant area was for food service.

Listen, all money is green, but rules are rules. The boss wanted me to get rid of them or move them into the bar. And I didn't want to get my face punched in. This was a situation I couldn't simply ignore until it went away.

I looked the guys over — they were huddled around the table, elbows resting on its surface, and deep in quiet conversation as they drank their beer. After quickly calculating a strategy, I casually walked over to the group, smiled and nodded, pulled a chair out, and sat down at their table. This immediately put me at their level in a nonthreatening — even vulnerable — position. I had brought a glass with me, and I nodded in respect to the group, set the glass down, and poured myself a small amount of beer. These were friendly gestures, not hostile ones. I leaned slightly forward, put one hand around the glass and rested the other on my thigh, and gave them a closed but humble smile. I said, "Guys, I have a problem."

"What's that?" one of them asked defiantly.

"Well," I continued, gesturing with my head toward the other side of the room, "my boss has a rule here that reserves the restaurant for food service. If you don't plan on ordering at least five dollars' worth of food, would you mind enjoying your beers and then leaving, as a favor to me?"

It worked. I could have come off as a hard-ass and gotten in trouble with both the bikers and the boss — not the reactions I was looking for. Instead, I presented myself as being in a predicament beyond my control, one these free spirits would understand — I was at the mercy of "the man." As I predicted, they weren't pissed off at all. They agreed to my terms and left when the pitcher was empty without breaking my nose. Happy ending. Think about all the things I had to do during that three-minute transaction: build rapport, project confidence, command respect without being aggressive, and bill myself as a relatable "poor schmuck" stuck within the conventions of his working-stiff life. Had I not had a plan, or not followed through with it, things might not have turned out so well.

There are times when you have to do unpleasant things, like talking to someone who has done something wrong or, worse, firing an employee who has failed to live up to standards you've set or failed to respond appropriately to your Reaction Management. These tasks are fraught with emotion for even the most practiced bosses. What do you do when you want to end a relationship in a reasonable and positive way? For this should be the goal of every termination. You do not want the other person to walk out and create an uncomfortable situation or even try to ruin you.

To turn around a failed employee who still has potential, I use something I call "personal reinforcement with professional correction." Like I said earlier, this is under normal circumstances, not *Bar Rescue* interventions. It always begins with a positive comment—and, indeed, every interaction that involves criticism should begin with a sincere compliment, because that disarms a person and sets him at ease.

For instance, I say, "I enjoy working with you, Howard, and your commitment to me and the company is unbelievable. I know we will get the job done. But there are a couple of things I want to talk to you about, where I really think your effort can be improved . . ." It's at this point that I tell him what's going on in terms of corrective measures. I've won his trust and anything I tell him now won't be met with much, if any, defensiveness.

The defensive reaction is not the one you're after when you want an employee to make improvements and change his work habits. You also have to provide genuine guidance; otherwise, the employee will just decide you're full of shit—and rightly so. "Do it better" doesn't cut it. If someone is not giving you what you want, you have to be as specific as possible. Otherwise resentment grows ("The boss is such a jerk. He tells me I'm not doing a good job, but he doesn't tell me how or why"). The manipulation must end with the person wanting to do better for you. If a manager and a good employee sit down for a correction or a disciplinary conversation and that employee leaves wanting to work for that boss *less,* who's the idiot?

As for letting someone go—that's a bit more difficult, of course, because few of us want to hurt people. I certainly don't like to hurt people. I want to be liked and respected, so firing is not a job I relish. However, hospitality work isn't for everyone. Bar work especially requires a certain personality and energy, so if you go into the business, be ready to fire some people because not everyone is going to work out.

That said, it's crucial that you let people go—people who have failed at nothing more than doing a specific job—with compassion. Know too that firing someone can often be the greatest kindness you can extend. Many successful people talk about being fired from the wrong job as a genuine catalyst to achieving greater things. Of course, this is a very difficult case to make with someone who is about to lose his livelihood; I get that. So the reactions of an employee who is being terminated have to be managed with great care.

> You have to take some of the heat when an employee must be terminated or a business partnership has to end. If your business has employees or partners who aren't a good fit, make no mistake, it is often because of your management skills, not market conditions ("good workers are impossible to find") or an employee's failings.

There are a number of people whom I have fired and then provided references for—for example, I fired a DJ who is now the music and stadium manager for an NBA team. He wasn't terminated because he was a lousy employee or a thief. He was just an awful DJ. If someone had wanted to hire him for that job, I couldn't in good conscience have recommended him. I *was* happy to recommend him for any other job because he was smart and dependable. It's not in my best interest to turn my back on good people. It robs them of dignity, and I can't do that. It's also a small world, and it could be beneficial to both sides to keep the lines of communication open.

"This is not personal," I say, "but you know as well as I do you are not the best at this job. You're not making as much in tips as the other servers, and I know you can tell that customers aren't always happy with your service—even though I've never gotten a complaint about your sincerity or effort. I've determined that you'd better off someplace else." More often than not, they agree, and sometimes they even express some relief. "What do you think you'd rather do?" I ask. "And how can I help? I'd be happy to provide references for the skills I know you do have." If you treat people that way and look in their faces with kindness, you'll be fine and they'll be fine. Good people need to be treated with dignity—it's your fault for hiring the wrong person; it's not the employee's fault for being the wrong person. That's humanity. When I send you out into the street, I want you to speak positively about me. That's just smart business.

Now, if I have to fire someone who is a thief—like a bartender taking money from the register or liquor from the pantry—that's an entirely different story. Then there is no discussion. There are no negotiations and no references. It's over. There should be no fear in getting rid of a threat to your business. All you have to say is: "You're terminated, effective immediately." Escort him or her to his or her locker to collect personal belongings. Let him or her know someone will be escorting him or her out the door. When someone is fired for a serious offense, there really is no point in having a conversation about "what went wrong."

## The Bucket List

Most people fall into one of four personality/motivational buckets: money, pride, ego, and fear. With a little practice, you'll be able to put people in the appropriate buckets and then play off their motivators for optimal Reaction Management. If you handle conversations correctly, most people will walk you into the right personality bucket on their own. It's not such a big deal; eventually it doesn't even take that much thought. As you will learn in chapter four, this is very useful when hiring staff.

"Really" and "and" are the two most important words in drawing out what's important to a person. It's tough to balance listening and responding, but take time to master it by learning to listen. You have to start somewhere, so you might say, "Did you see that Yankee game the other night?" How he responds cues your next question. If he says, "Yeah, that was something," you might say, "Do you play sports yourself?" If he says, "I used to play," or "I coach my son's Little League team," start using "really" and "and" to get him to open up. Attune yourself to where he takes the conversation, particularly the topics, issues, or ideas that recur. Persistent themes are valuable information.

Someone who is motivated by money often talks about the size of his house or the brand of his car, or the fact that he's been working since he was sixteen. He may also talk about his work history or accomplishments in terms of economics. The ego-driven person is often conscious of status and will talk about his life in terms of symbols of success. He will talk about promotions earned or awards won. However, the person in the fear bucket may cross his arms when I'm describing certain jobs; this immediately tells me he's resistant and perhaps uncomfortable with risk and the unknown. He may avoid discussing certain subjects or practice denial.

Bill Rodenhiser bought the Chicken Bone in Framingham, Massachusetts, as a way of doing something he thought he would love (running a bar) and getting away from his successful but unsatisfying excavation business. When I met Bill, the bar had sales of $2 million a year but it was *losing* so much money, it was facing possible bankruptcy. Money was a problem, but Bill's real bucket was fear — he had already been forced to sell his big, beautiful home and move his lovely family into a small condo many miles away from where he worked. I discuss the mechanics of the Chicken Bone turnaround in chapter five, but the way I got Bill to see his business differently was by appealing to his fear of losing everything, including not only all his money but also his family. Before we began the rescue, I was pretty blunt with Bill that if he did not take my advice, everything he worked for and invested in would disappear.

When I went to talk about *Bar Rescue* with Spike TV, I understood the hot button was pride — the network wanted a show it could be proud of. I knew it was a male-oriented station with aggressive, in-your-face television shows, but Spike also wanted respect. I could help give it that with a "smart" reality program that would offer information of benefit to viewers — entertaining them as well, of course. I showed conviction with the bar and restaurant science I had access to, and I hooked Spike's executives with that. It helped manipulate them to commit to a pilot because they were curious; they sensed that what I was offering was a show that had both integrity and drama.

Customers also fall into one of these four buckets, so I ensure businesses I work with have programs in place to appeal to various personality types: a program that highlights cost savings appeals to money personalities; those that help a customer feel good about themselves appeals to pride; "VIP" marketing programs make some customers feel as though they have achieved high status with the company; and creating a level of comfort helps fearful or insecure customers feel at ease trying a business for the first time.

My definition of good management is the achievement of objectives through the manipulation of others. Let's stop saying that manipulation is not what we do. It *is* what we do. Embrace manipulation and get better at it; be deliberate to achieve the best results for everyone. So let me ask you—how would you change your interactions with people now that you know you're always causing reactions and that you can manipulate those reactions to your benefit?

3

# Money Is in Reactions, Not Transactions

> There is only one boss. The customer. And he can fire everybody in the company from the chairman on down, simply by spending his money somewhere else.
>
> — SAM WALTON, FOUNDER, WALMART

IF YOU THINK OF TRANSACTIONS purely as financial exchanges, you're missing a big piece of the picture. Every transaction you have with the public should be a building block in a long and profitable relationship. Transactions are any kind of exchange you have that promotes and enhances your business, including offering goods or services for money, providing excellent customer service, or being a good neighbor to win acceptance from the community you're in. Every transaction has to feel personal and be pleasantly memorable if you want them to lead to repeat customers, referrals, and community acceptance.

Angry Ham's Garage in Framingham, Massachusetts, offers a perfect example of how to fail at customer transactions, but also how to turn them around. First off, in case you're wondering, Angry Ham's is a bar, not an auto shop. Tim Hanna, the owner, built the place along with two friends, former professional hockey player for the Boston Bruins Lyndon "L.B." Byers and Richard Oleson, as a monument to themselves, not their customers. The name says it all — every worker was angry, which made customers feel unwelcome, as though they were intruding on a private club. In fact, it's common knowledge among Framingham locals that "ham" is an insult; residents don't take kindly to the term.

The name might have been a bigger turnoff than the owner was willing to admit; the bar didn't entice many potential customers. Online reviews were dismal: "Our waitress took our drink order and served them right away . . . but disappeared for twenty minutes. We finally ordered a burger but the waitress pulled her disappearing act again. We didn't see her for well over a half hour . . . we wanted to order more drinks but she was nowhere to be found."

We talked to people on the street and common reactions included "I avoid the place," "It seems dangerous," or, simply, "Ham's — ugh, I'd never go in there." The owners were having a tough time developing a good relationship with community leaders. Bars have to be especially conscious of the way they fit into a neighborhood, especially if they're in close proximity to residential areas — Angry Ham's was near a retirement home. People are naturally concerned with late-night noise, rowdy crowds at closing time, and unpleasant sanitary conditions. Sometimes you have to bend over backward to demonstrate the bar is an asset to the neighborhood, not a drawback.

A big issue for Angry Ham's was its association with L.B. — one of the Bruins' "frequent fighters" who was known more for violent altercations with rival team members than for winning plays on the ice. That reputation followed him to Angry Ham's. Bruins fans might have enjoyed watching L.B. fight on TV, from the safety of their living rooms, but few wanted to chance dealing with him in the flesh.

I sent chef Brian Duffy in to check out Angry Ham's one evening, and the dining room was completely empty. This confirmed the lack of interest I had heard from the community. It's hard to have a transaction, even a bad one, when there's no one around to have a transaction with. The customers who had ventured through the door of the bar, including Brian, were greeted with cocktail waitresses playing darts and drinking with each other. It took more than fifteen minutes for Brian to place an order and just as long to receive it.

Customers say that slow service and inattentive servers are the two most unpleasant experiences they have in a bar or a restaurant—again highlighting that transactions in the hospitality business are *taken personally.*

Up to 68 percent of customers who see workers goofing off, instead of helping them, react by telling family and friends about the bad experience and posting about it on social media. Another 35 percent of neglected customers say the treatment is enough to end their relationship with a business. More than 60 percent of people who see or hear negative comments are influenced not to give the establishment a chance. So not only does a business lose a current customer, but it also loses potential new ones. Angry Ham's was a case study in these effects.

I hired beverage-auditing firm Bevintel to measure liquor use behind the bar and discovered that in just four days the staff had given away nearly $3,000 in liquor. No surprise there: employees freely poured themselves drinks without paying for them and deliberately over-poured customers' drinks to elicit better tips. And owner Tim Hanna wasn't particularly upset by the negative transactions his staff was creating because he'd hired his friends to work for him. For some bizarre reason he wanted them to have a good time during their shifts.

Believe me, I'm a huge proponent of happy staff members who enjoy their jobs — happy employees create a sense of fun for the customer, and that results in happy transactions. But I want them to actually do their jobs. Hanna lacked the discipline to tighten his ship, which was ironic considering he did have good restaurant experience and, in fact, came from a family of restaurant people.

Bottom line — there were other changes that needed to take place at Angry Ham's, but chief among them was bringing the staff up to a professional standard and have employees take customer service seriously. Hanna also had to distance L.B. from the business — it was one of the important keys to convincing the community board that the business wanted to be a positive member of the city. We taught the staff — cocktail waitresses, bartenders, and servers — to welcome guests as soon as they walked in, take their order quickly and with a smile, and deliver orders in less than fifteen minutes. The staff also refrained from goofing off on the job, particularly in front of customers; breaks, for example, should not be taken in front of the patrons.

Even though the bar ended up keeping its name (which I still believe they should have permanently changed) and tossing some of the décor we installed during the makeover, bar sales and profits still increased in the months after the rescue. This demonstrates that customer transactions are key in promoting loyalty. Angry Ham's started to build repeat business. New reviews were much kinder: "I came to Angry Ham's for post-game drinks with coworkers Thursday evening. The bartender was wonderful, attentive and quick," and "the staff is very friendly."

A friendly person who smiles and says hello, takes an order, and quickly serves a refreshing cocktail in the appropriate glass is not all that different from a salesperson helping a shopper find the perfect dress or an airline representative finding you the best deal on the best seat for a cross-country flight. Individual transactions that make for a great experience leave a lasting impression that can and does promote business. They can also overcome other shortcomings, whether intentional (as in the case of Angry Ham's) or unintentional errors that happen in businesses every day. We are very forgiving when we perceive that an effort has been made to be friendly, welcoming, and caring.

Great customer reactions are more important than any marketing vehicle. To test this premise at a restaurant I owned, I reduced marketing and promotional expenses over a six-month period and reinvested those dollars into "experiences" and customer "transactions"—great service, entertainment, events, contests, tastings, and so on. Over six months, I increased guest frequency by more than two visits a month and increased revenue by over 24 percent. Rather than radio relationships, I had guest relationships. This changed the way I viewed marketing and the guest experience. Invest in guest reactions, not in media.

## The Brutalization of Service in America

Mechanical transactions are fine if you're only interested in doing single or unique sales. A newsstand in a busy airport can survive this way because it has a captive and ever-changing audience. Bars are different—they need both regulars and new customers to thrive. You have to build your business through transactions that maximize the guest experience and increase spending frequency. My own research statistics tell me that even with the best service in the world, the odds are not in our favor. When people visit a bar or restaurant for the first time and have a great experience, fewer than 50 percent return because the establishment is not in their life pattern or habit cycle — and that's under ideal transactional circumstances. So we know that one positive visit does not make for a steady customer.

The second time a person visits a bar or restaurant, there is a 50 percent chance he will return. The third time he comes, there is a 70 percent chance he will come back a fourth time. When I teach staff members to make transactions count, I am teaching them to work for that third visit; likewise, when I market to new customers, I am really marketing for their third, not their first, visit. This is why transactions have to be held to a high standard and remain consistent and, to a great extent, predictable. It's nice to be surprised by superior service, but once you've set the bar that high, you have to deliver on it every time. It's equally surprising but more disastrous for a customer to have a negative transaction, especially when they were expecting something quite different.

> Increasing guest frequency by just one visit a month increases revenue up to 12 percent.

Quality service motivates consumers. Once a repeat customer sees that service standards are consistent, he is much more likely to return for a third and fourth visit. Unfortunately, for the most part we're still living in the Dark Ages of customer service. In the last decade, service has deteriorated quantitatively and qualitatively to the point where it's barbaric how most companies regularly deal with consumers. As a customer, I don't want to have to work at a transaction, answering twenty questions or providing copious proof of my existence. I do not want to have to beg a business to take my money.

This sorry state of affairs infects all kinds of businesses; it's not limited to the hospitality industry. Financial and government institutions, utility companies, telemarketers, insurance providers, retail stores, and most other sectors of the economy often treat customers as herds of faceless wallets. This indifference or aloofness no doubt costs them loyalty and repeat customers. Businesses have placed their need for efficiencies and shareholder earnings before customer needs. Everyone loses: consumers, companies, owners, investors, and shareholders. Good employees suffer too, since low expectations create a vicious cycle of "If you're going to treat me like crap, why should I bother?" When customers are rude to employees — even when it appears to be "justified" — it lowers worker morale, affects the mental health of employees, and can lead to destructive behavior such as employee theft and property destruction.

A few examples: Take what I call "the loop," a company's customer service phone tree. Most quickly lead a caller deep into a system where he or she is asked to hold, press another button, or state a service category. If you make a mistake, you have to back up and start again. Once people become accustomed to a phone tree's vagaries, the company changes them (e.g., pressing "o" no longer gets you the operator; pressing "#" does) and you are warned that you must listen carefully "because the options have changed." The common response is to hang up the phone in frustration. No evidence shows such phone systems live up to their claim "to better serve you." In fact, customer polls show the opposite.

The legacy airlines are the barbarians at the gate. Nearly every traveler you meet has at least one airline service horror story, and probably more. Employees walk off the job to take their designated breaks when passenger lines snake into the distance. Human-computer interaction makes transactions in these circumstances atrocious. The endless clatter of keyboards as the attendant glowers at the monitor, ignoring you, carries on as you wait and wait and wait. All you wanted was an aisle seat. Fifteen or twenty years ago, I had a loyalty to United even though it was more expensive than the other airlines. The company sent me a holiday card annually, and once it even sent me a CD with seasonal music. But over the years United, along with other airlines, started to struggle and in the process made transactions mechanical and impersonal. Those attempts at forging a relationship with me disappeared, so now I fly on whatever airline is convenient, aside from a couple of carriers I refuse to fly with.

Poor service actually seems to be part of an airline strategy to intentionally steer passengers to websites to purchase tickets and away from telephone representatives. This keeps customers away from booking personnel to save airlines labor costs and travel agency commissions. In essence, the airline thinks it is winning through poor service, because it's moving you to its website, which lowers its costs. The overall result is that customer choice is now based only upon the cheapest fare. Despite charging extra fees for checked baggage, extra legroom in some coach seats, and, in some cases, pillows and blankets, airline profits have been in a consistent slump.

At $8.4 billion, global profits in 2011 were half of what they were in 2010. Worldwide profits in 2012 were about $4.1 billion. Although the airlines could survive even if the American economy continues to limp along and demand for air travel increases only incrementally, fuel costs and global economic issues have the potential to cause more economic catastrophe that could further damage the industry. Customer loyalty and quality service are the key assets airlines need to solve their problems, but they're the exact assets that most airlines have abandoned! Wouldn't you be willing to pay more and even travel by air more frequently if you knew that all the transactions involved in booking and taking a flight were going to be pleasant? I know I would.

Unfortunately, research shows that restaurants have the highest frequency of rude service encounters or transactions, with 83 percent of the respondents in one study saying that a restaurant server or staff member was rude to them at some point during a visit. The same percentage of people said they witnessed one restaurant employee be rude to a colleague or subordinate. We have to get better at teaching employees conflict resolution, how to deal with fussy guests, and how to handle high-stress situations like busy periods or shifts that are short of staff.

Here's how those dynamics often play out: Even if an employee is empowered to solve a customer's problems, the employee's "people skills" aren't sufficiently developed to the point where he can read a customer's emotional responses and react appropriately and successfully. Customers often experience such interactions as "worse than poor service" or as "a frustrating encounter" or being "disrespected." Owners not only have to train their people better in human relations, but they also have to become more astute at spotting a transaction about to go south and intervene before it deteriorates. This is one more compelling reason to manage from "front to back."

Consumers are more sensitive to the quality of transactions they have because they're simply more educated and aware of what quality service can and should be. Americans regularly tour the globe and experience high levels of service delivered in other regions of the world, most notably in Asia, where the concept of quality service is actively practiced. When we see and encounter fine service, we understandably want to experience the same at home, in the course of our everyday lives.

The best companies in every sector create customer relationships based on trust and high customer expectations. Nowadays, great personal service is, in itself, a standalone point of difference. Zappos, the online shoe and clothing retailer, works hard to make its customer transactions better than its competitors'. Luxury carmaker Lexus consistently outpaces other makers of high-end cars in terms of customer satisfaction. Southwest Airlines has built its business on customer service and direct human interaction. Call the company yourself and find out. Unlike many other airlines, it's fairly easy to get right to a real person who speaks understandable English. The fewer barriers to making a human connection, the better.

Each Ritz-Carlton hotel makes a daily practice of meeting to discuss every guest's needs before he arrives so that the staff is prepared to anticipate him; every transaction is optimized for the guest. If you are a vegetarian or vegan, every meal served reflects this. If you need extra towels, there is no limit to how many will be supplied. The company's credo, "We are Ladies and Gentlemen serving Ladies and Gentleman," says it all. Those words define the kind of transactions you expect to have when you go to a Ritz-Carlton property. It's a maxim that defines who is hired and how they are trained, and the kind of service they extend to guests.

Companies with operating philosophies that seek financial results by providing superior human transactions rather than the promise of convenience through technology always win. Brand, business, or product loyalty comes from human interactions and transactions, *not* from the conveniences of technology. These smart companies know that their financial futures lie in the memorable and beneficial transactions they create with their customers. They are among the leaders in the service renaissance in great part because they have made the customer transaction a winning value proposition. Knowing this gives your bar an advantage. You know where to invest your money, staff, and time.

So why don't more companies demand the best customer service practices? Three major forces have devastated customer service. First, computerization and automation of transactions have had a dehumanizing effect on the core aspects of service. Let's remember that customer service is an interpersonal experience; it doesn't come from "press or say one." That's a very forgettable transaction, even when it works well, which isn't very often. I have never, not once, heard anyone say, "Jon, I have got to tell you about this amazing phone tree experience I had the other day . . ." ATM machines provide access and convenience but fail as a customer service experience. Technological conveniences distance the consumer from business; positive human interaction cultivates consumer loyalty.

Second, the "wired generation" has pioneered lives where relationships occur more readily online than in person. It's great that people are digitally savvy, but it's not good for businesses to have a pool of employees who are more comfortable interacting through IM and Facebook than face-to-face. Employers have discovered that many members of the wired generation lack real-time interpersonal skills essential to developing positive in-person customer transactions. Businesses are now in the position of having to train employees on how to interact with "real" customers. The problem is that traditional training methods are time-consuming and expensive and don't create the kinds of transactions that produce the reactions necessary for a return on investment. I don't even like to use the word "training" because it makes me think of a seal in a circus doing tricks for the audience. I do talk at length about teaching employees elsewhere in the book, but I reiterate here that you need to help employees understand that customer service is an emotional experience for the guest. Expectations and emotions are closely linked in a customer's mind, and the more the experience deviates from the expectation, the more negative the emotion becomes. Simply reframing it this way goes a long way to illuminating how important human interaction is to the *employee's* success—he or she will earn better tips and encourage regulars to go out of their way to be served by that employee in the future.

Third, the growing demand on employees that labor cuts have necessitated does strain the camel's back. The continued rise in the social costs of doing business, such as health-care benefits, has reduced the workforce, especially in small companies forced to keep head count and revenues at a certain level in order to keep expenses, tax obligations, and regulatory requirements to a minimum. Companies have trimmed budgets and want to operate on a leaner, more flexible business platform. In short, there are fewer employees with less training doing more work. Some of this work requires human interaction for which they have no training or sensitivity. This can make for some stressful work situations.

To lift service out of its dark dungeon and bring about a Service Renaissance in America, companies must realize that service is a transaction. It can be a real point of distinction that doesn't actually cost a lot of money. In effect, every company's product is a vehicle to positive customer reactions. From this perspective, American Airlines would no longer sell seats, and Sprint would not sell telephone services. The seat on the plane and the reception on a phone are only delivery systems of an experience that the customer gets from the transactions. These transactions are, in fact, the "product" that causes future revenue growth.

Can it be done? Yes, quantitatively and qualitatively. For example, a few years ago a famous hotel in California earned a chilling "Second Worst in Service" rating in a company-wide guest satisfaction survey. By implementing a solid "human reactions"–based training and service policy, the hotel turned around customer opinions in *one* quarter by making sure its staff understood that every transaction with a customer counted.

## Heroes of the Reactional Transaction Experience

There are a few individuals who have proved that the reactions customers have to business transactions are an essential ingredient for success. Walt Disney was a complex person full of contradictions, but as an innovative entrepreneur he broke ground. When he opened Disneyland in 1955, his credit cards were maxed out. Women's high heels sank into the blacktop during the opening days because he hadn't had enough money to lay parking lots far enough in advance to cure thoroughly. Despite the glitches, Disneyland was a success because Walt Disney understood the value and potential of LBE, or location-based entertainment. Sure, there were arcades and amusement parks before Disneyland, but by applying the ideas of entertainment and show business to the amusement park business, Disney elevated consumer transactions and made them that much more emotional and exciting — and profitable.

Walt Disney was the first to call employees "cast members," workstations "stages," uniforms "costumes," and rides "attractions." Transactions were not limited to buying a ticket for an attraction, getting on and off it, and then buying a hot dog. The park was a totally integrated experience, and transactions were varied and always new and fresh — from meeting favorite characters on the "street," to eating in special interactive restaurants, to climbing aboard an exciting attraction. Disney's premises are at the heart of everything I do. The makeovers on *Bar Rescue* always integrate service with food, drinks, ambiance, décor, traffic patterns, and lighting, creating a holistic experience for the customer.

So many hospitality and retail companies use some version of the Disney philosophy today — from theme parks such as Universal Studios, to restaurants such as Chuck E. Cheese's, to retailers such as Apple and even AT&T. (In August 2012, AT&T opened a ten-thousand-square-foot experiential flagship store in Chicago with an Apps Bar staffed by "app-tenders" and communal spaces to sit and play with gadgets.) "Experiential retailing" and "experiential hospitality" are direct descendants of LBE. Destination venues must offer exciting transactions to consumers — people visit them specifically to engage in the transactional experiences they offer. There's a lot bars can learn from this.

You have to offer people the opportunity to engage in a host of desirable transactions, beyond what is required to acquire a drink or a basket of chicken wings. It's far more important for location-based businesses like bars to understand this than it was in the 1950s and 1960s. People have many more entertainment choices today that don't require a car trip or a stroll into town — social media and online interaction are taking up more and more of people's time. Nielsen reports that the average American spends about 23 percent of her Internet time on social networks. It found that the average Facebook user spent seven hours per month on the site in 2010, up from four hours and thirty-nine minutes in 2009. Experian reports that more than 66 percent of Americans online used social-networking sites in 2010, up from 20 percent in 2007. Unless you make a transaction enticing enough that someone will want to go out of his way to experience it, you will find it extremely challenging to be successful in the hospitality or the retail business.

Hugh Hefner was one of the great masters of mechanical dynamics. Although there are no longer any Playboy Clubs, he developed an idea that is still used by successful restaurants and nightclubs today. At the clubs Hefner created, cocktail waitresses, called Bunnies, were trained in every detail: how to stand, walk, bend, take orders, lean, shake hands, talk to customers, pick up something that had fallen, serve food and drink. This careful choreography made for an incredibly appealing and novel transaction for customers, who may never in their lives have experienced service in quite this way.

This approach was very pioneering in its day, and you can see the remnants of it if you've ever ventured into Hooters, which, don't get me wrong, is no Playboy Club. However, the Hooters company has appearance specs that include Skechers sneakers, shorts worn with panty hose, and branded tank tops. The company specifically defines what servers should look like so that individual characteristics do not stand out. Service standards are also set in stone — it's very rare to interact with a Hooters Girl who doesn't smile and laugh and make you feel like she's been waiting for your arrival with great anticipation. The specifics of the concept may have begun to feel dated, but the idea behind them, the mechanics that help consumers predict and expect a certain kind of transaction, is timeless.

You can't talk about transactions without mentioning Ray Kroc, the founder of the McDonald's franchise. Kroc understood that he was not in the burger business; he was in the franchise business. He created a system that offered almost immediate "mastery" to someone with no restaurant experience. The system was designed to enable unskilled sixteen-year-old kids and elderly people with no food service experience to master their jobs as food preparers. At the time, this was really a miracle. So well executed is the McDonald's franchise system that it's possible to walk into one anywhere in the world and expect and receive a very similar transaction. This is why there are so many McDonald's loyalists — the expectation and the experience rarely diverge.

The benefit of the transaction, and what makes McDonald's so successful, is its ability to quickly deliver consistent, tasty food to cash- and time-strapped people who want to get out of the house once in a while and "eat out." Now, I know that some of you could probably tell me a nightmarish experience you've had at a McDonald's over the course of your lives. But these are anomalies compared to the number of franchises in the world (more than thirty-two thousand) and the billions of orders that McDonald's has filled over the years. Customers are much more likely to blame a particular franchise or a specific employee for a poor experience, rather than the company as a whole. One bad experience rarely leads a McDonald's customer to sever ties with the company. If negative experiences were common, McDonald's stock would not consistently perform well no matter the economic conditions, and stock experts wouldn't regularly include the company on their "pick lists."

## Predictably Great

Kroc accomplished something that had never been done in the industry before. By mastering the concept of front-end planning, he created a business that could offer predictable transactions as soon as a new McDonald's opened its doors to the public. This, to me, is the key to great transactions — as soon as you learn what to expect and you like it, you want to have the same experience from that company every time. I like to support local businesses in today's economy, but I have to admit that when I'm in strange city and I have a choice between a Capital Grille and, say, "Lou's Steak House," Capital Grille wins almost every time. I know what to expect and I expect to get it; a good meal is nearly guaranteed.

Lou's could be the greatest place in the world, but sometimes, and maybe too often, we sacrifice the possibility of excellence for predictability. National brands have an advantage over local brands in that they create "known certainty." Starbucks creates a consistent transaction experience in its coffeehouses. Walk into any Starbucks anywhere in the country and it's easy to make yourself at home. You know where everything is, you know how the line functions, you know where the sandwiches are kept and how the coffee is prepared and served. While maintaining consistency, Starbucks also actively looks for ways to ramp up customer transactions with unexpected delights.

One impressive Starbucks transaction involved baristas handing small folded cards to customers sitting at tables. The front side of the car read "Spread Summer Sunshine." When you flipped the card over, the following was printed: "Somebody's going to do something nice for you today. Maybe they'll let you go first in the register line. Maybe they'll give you some change so you don't have to break a twenty. Or maybe they'll just hold the door for you when your hands are full. Whatever the nice thing turns out to be, return the favor by giving that anonymous benefactor this card. You'll both find a little Karma goes a long way. This card is good for a Banana Coconut or Bananas & Crème Frappuccino blended beverage." Now that is a very cool transaction because it makes customers think, promotes more transactions, and gets customers to participate in creating them.

At this point you may be thinking, "How does this apply to me? I've got one storefront. I don't have a big brand yet. I can work on my customer transactions, but give me a break—how do I make them widely known and appreciated?" One customer at a time—when I talked earlier about the statistics of repeat customers, that's what small business owners have to focus on. Create individual transactions that lead to that third and fourth visit. While it's true that national brands have the advantage of familiarity, this doesn't mean you can't model their delivery and consistency promises. Your advantage is uniqueness—a customer can only get the experience you offer from *you.*

If you think this is a problem, consider Mystique Lounge in West Palm Beach, Florida, which was, when I visited, living on a legacy of one very bad transaction. New owners Torres Anwar and Darren Cummings tried to turn the nightclub around three years after a 2009 murder, the result of a deadly fight that had taken place right outside the venue. The violence had crippled Mystique's business, and when I arrived on the scene the place drew troublesome, rowdy crowds.

Gone were the high-end, fun-loving patrons who had moved on to safer and more urbane venues.

The owners had tried to turn the nightclub around by hiring John, a young club promoter. Because Anwar and Cummings were inexperienced and desperate to draw a better clientele to the club, they made a crazy deal with John: they agreed to give him 100 percent of the door profits. They hoped to rely on drink sales and bottle service to make a profit. (Bottle service is when you bring an entire bottle of liquor to a table — and charge many times the retail price for the privilege.) Beverage sales numbers were half of the initial take, once the cover charge was deducted and handed over to John. Meanwhile, John's promoting did nothing to shift the audience from unruly and violent to sophisticated and civilized; the nightclub continued to lose money.

When I met the two owners, they were $80,000 in debt and trying to cope with weekly losses of $2,500. The club's customer transactions were awful. There were no standards. Cleanliness, staff training, even the glassware and napkins were terrible. Taffer team member and service pro Jessie Barnes went undercover as a customer along with a few friends. They requested VIP bottle service and were shown to a special section of tables Jessie described as "toilets without buckets." The carafe of orange juice she ordered with a bottle of vodka came out accessorized with human hair. The girls sent it back and another carafe came, this one dirty. When Jessie pointed that out to the waitress, she actually countered Jessie's complaint with the argument that the dirt was "on the outside" of the pitcher. It was on the inside, not that it mattered. This was a very bad customer transaction indeed. Then, on my inspection, I found multiple standard cleaning practices had been completely ignored, including hooking up the sanitation chemicals to the dishwasher.

All good customer transactions are built on a foundation of operating standards. Without them, and I go into depth on this in chapter eight, transactions can never be consistent or reliable. The germ-infested bar was so filthy, I insisted that the entire staff clean it from top to bottom before anything else happened.

Jessie taught the staff how to serve a $200 bottle of vodka so that high-end customers would have their expectations met (and return for more on a subsequent evening). It's all about making the guest feel special at that level of expenditure. Presentation is everything. Jessie showed the staff how to present the bottles and accoutrements, such as the napkins, stir sticks, ice bucket, and extra glasses. The little things make the experience special: don't put a bottle in the same ice that is intended to go in a drink, place the glasses on a clean napkin in an appealing formation, and, most important, use clean glasses and serving pieces. Taffer team mixologist Joe Meyer emphasized the importance of consistent drink recipes, proper pour techniques, garnishing, and matching glassware to type of drink.

We also changed the tables and seating in the VIP bottle area to create a visual impression that bottle service would be comfortable and elegant. Tiered tables and decorative features previously absent invited patrons to settle in and stay longer. A custom lighting system enriched the space and made the experience flattering to female customers, as well as sexy and romantic for everyone.

For this bar, the details that reinforced good service transactions were only half of the story. For any bar to truly succeed — and for this one in particular — it must provide a safe environment. I helped this along by properly training the door staff and security guards. Mandating dress codes, teaching proper door protocol, and opening up communication with local authorities so that potentially negative situations could be diffused before they got out of hand went a long way toward assuring customers before they even entered the nightclub that they would have a pleasant and safe evening once inside.

The reopening of the renamed Aura Nightclub provided a new, positive energy that the owners and staff feel proud of. Bartenders now serve balanced, fresh, properly poured cocktails, while the bottle servers elevate guest experience through their newly acquired skills. In terms of perception, patrons are pleased with the positive theme and the far more comfortable, safer surroundings. Three months after the launch, bar and bottle sales had gone up substantially, and the venue had been free of any negative or unruly incidents. The positive customer transactions have led to repeat customers, and the owners have begun to reach the critical mass — those third and fourth visits — they need to sustain the business for the long haul.

By focusing on what the local audience wants and providing it consistently every time, Aura is building a reputation for great customer experiences. There is no reason, if the owners are successful with this bar, that Anwar and Cummings couldn't build Aura into a major brand. I might be getting ahead of myself (and them) because creating sustained success takes time, money, and commitment. But the fact is, once you understand how to create great transaction reactions, and teach staff to do so, the Promised Land is within your reach.

# 4

# Employees, the Engine of Reaction Management

Motivation is everything. You can do the work of two people, but you can't be two people. Instead, you have to inspire the next guy down the line and get him to inspire his people.

— LEE IACOCCA, *IACOCCA: AN AUTOBIOGRAPHY*

EXECUTIVE CHEF KEITH DENARD JONES strolled into Weber's Place in Reseda, California, one evening in mid-2012. Keith is trained in classical French methods, but that doesn't mean he can't appreciate great bar food, like a plate of wings with spicy dipping sauce. Unfortunately, neither was served at Weber's that night—or any other night in the bar's recent history. The 2,800-square-foot venue was only moderately busy when Keith dropped by, yet it was staffed to the max. Several barmaids and servers, along with a bartender and a manager, were all on duty. The bar's owner, Kervin Cinton, was also on the premises. Despite the surfeit of help, after sitting down at the bar, Keith had to proactively recruit someone to take this order.

"Would it be possible for me to get a menu?" Keith asked Rodiah, a server preoccupied with snapping her fingers to the beat of the band onstage.

"Yup," she replied, without making eye contact. "What can I get for you?"

"I'll have a dry martini and the wings with sauce on the side," Keith said. Rodiah scooped ice from the freezer with a glass and prepared the cocktail. She served the drink fairly quickly, and it was okay except that it was over-poured and way too strong. (And luckily, the drink didn't have any bits of glass sitting in it. Scooping up ice with a glass is a rookie mistake and incredibly dangerous since glass can break. No one, not even the most seasoned bar pro, can tell the difference between shards of ice and shards of glass.)

Twenty minutes later, Keith was still waiting for his wings.

"I was trying to send up a signal, hoping that someone would notice and come over to ask if everything was okay," Keith told me. No such luck—Rodiah and her colleagues were too busy dancing behind the bar and ignoring customers. Keith could have fallen off his stool and not one employee would have noticed.

A few minutes after that, bar owner Kervin suggested to Rodiah that she was "supposed to be working."

"I'm not working," she answered casually, continuing to dance. Somehow, between dancing and schmoozing with her colleagues, Rodiah did get Keith's food ticket into the kitchen. Van, the cook, shuffled around in front of the fryer bins before grabbing raw wings from a cooler. Her disorganization was mind-blowing, especially since she had just this one order to prepare.

The raw wings were stacked about six or seven inches high in a tall bucket that sat in melting ice, a bad sign since food stored four or more inches high cannot get cool enough to comply with health codes that require cold storage to be no more than 40 degrees. Van put the wings in a fry basket before plunging them into dark, sediment-filled oil. When they were done, plated, and placed on the service shelf (a pair of giant red lips sticking out from the wall), Rodiah interrupted her dance performance to serve Keith his wings. For clarification, go-go dancing was not actually part of Rodiah's job description, and judging from the customers' complete disinterest in her gyrations, it shouldn't have been.

"I opened one wing and immediately saw that there had been something very wrong with the temperature of the chicken before it went into the oil," Keith told me. "The meat was discolored and had a rubbery texture. I couldn't bring myself to even try one." The dipping sauce looked like red glue.

Okay, enough. I'd been watching the entire episode from a video screen in my car. It was time for me to check in with Kervin to find out what the hell was going on. I knew he had bought the former strip club in 2007 with most of his savings in hopes of bringing it back to its former 1980s glory as a hot spot for emerging bands. It wasn't quite working out as planned. It's difficult to book really good bands when you're just a few miles away from some of the best music venues in Los Angeles, including the Whisky a Go Go, the Troubadour, and the Viper Room. When Kervin did manage to score a group that had built a following, it would be out of that place faster than a drum roll, headed for hipper, bigger spots with better stages and reputations.

Kervin's business plan regarding live music made absolutely no sense to me. But what was really shocking was his inability to manage a staff that had clearly gone into a tailspin. The kitchen and bar areas followed no protocol of cleanliness, storage, safety, or quality and quantity controls. For instance, we checked the temperature of the "cooler" where the raw wings and other food were kept, and found it was a toasty and dangerous 72 degrees. There were other sanitation lapses in the kitchen as well—days-old chicken blood sitting in a tub, built-up grime in the walk-in refrigerator—despite the fact that Van had a state certification in food safety.

More devastating?

"They all steal from me," Kervin told me matter-of-factly, in what was an incredibly candid admission about his employees.

Here's a guy who recognized his bar wasn't being properly maintained and who *knew* his employees were pilfering both cash and liquor. His solution?

"I'm trying to train them not to be thieves."

In the hospitality business you're dealing with the public in an intimate way—providing products that are consumed. Food safety can be life-and-death, so failure can't be tolerated.

Stealing is nothing new in the bar business—it happens all the time. Theft was rampant at Barney's Beanery and the Troubadour before I put an end to it.

"Do you really think you can teach people who steal not to steal?" I asked Kervin. "Do you think that someone who steals today won't steal tomorrow?"

"Yes, I think I can rehabilitate people," he told me. His theory—stay with me here—was that at least he knew who was working for him. If he fired the entire staff and hired new people, how would he know if they weren't thieves too?

Kervin knew why he was losing money and chose to do nothing about it. In fact, his workers characterized him as a "nice guy" — code for "patsy" — and they freely took advantage of his overly forgiving and nonconfrontational nature. Weber's Place had devolved to the point where no one on payroll had any respect for the owner.

When I told the staff members they'd be working for me for five days while we tried to get Weber's back in the black, Rodiah didn't take too kindly to my stance.

"He needs to pipe it down when he's dealing with me," she told one of my producers, "unless he wants to get his face rearranged." That was the first time a woman had ever threatened me with bodily harm. Rodiah didn't mince words with me either. "Pipe down, player," she said, when I laid down the ground rules for the makeover and told them what would be expected from the staff. "Don't be fucking disrespectful, homey." This was going to be one challenging turnaround.

The staff dragging Weber's down the rabbit hole was the direct result of flawed hiring, absent procedural controls, missing standards, and low expectations. It's ironic that such a profoundly people-oriented business often has so many staffing issues. Every failing bar I've worked with — Weber's, Angry Ham's, Mystique, or any of the hundreds of others I've helped over the years — can attribute its imminent collapse to workers who are undereducated in the demands of the job, have no concept or knowledge of rules (if rules exist at all), have little respect for the owner or manager, and have no quantifiable way to measure or judge their performance.

Successful bars, like many businesses, need to mesh hierarchy, establish strong leadership that provides clear direction and vision at the same time fostering teamwork, while also encouraging good employees to develop as they succeed through merit-based reward systems.

The common denominator I see is that the owners or managers of these businesses think of their workers as "family." What a mistake. Successful businesses have winning *teams* that promote and encourage winning players and mitigate weakness through peer pressure. Teams work together on clear objectives that force individual members to perform or leave. If a batter strikes out all the time, his team will use various forms of coercion to make him try harder and do better. If the quarterback stinks, he can't contribute to a winning game. A lousy second baseman isn't going to stop enough double plays. If these players display chronic limitations game after game, their days are numbered. The coach can't afford to keep them around—the weakest players must be eliminated.

Families, on the other hand, protect and coddle their weakest members; often they enable relatives who might be better off with a kick in the pants. But it is the nature of families to shield the vulnerable and excuse the faint of heart. That's why the expression "we're like family here" drives me crazy: it suggests a dysfunctional organization. In a work setting, the "cancer of nurturing" promotes paying attention to weak employees while ignoring stellar performers because you think they don't "need" you. That's rewarding exactly the wrong person. What you get in return is a poor performer who does not improve and a frustrated and resentful talented worker who will eventually quit or perhaps exact revenge in some other way. Never allow social or familial motivations to take priority over business objectives.

Profitable bars, like any well-run business, play on the strengths and talents of employees and minimize weaknesses through proper guidance or elimination. If you can't rally your team and create energy, enthusiasm, honesty, and reliability, you'll struggle. Employees justify themselves or they will be fired. Life is too short and business is too competitive to take any other attitude. Kervin was failing on all counts. His problem employees would have to go, the honest few would have to relearn their jobs, and, most important, the right new people would have to be brought in. There's simply no excuse for a lousy staff. The economic downturn and increased unemployment in other fields has actually freed up potential workers. For years small or weak labor pools did plague some sectors of our industry, but no more. Today you can find outstanding employees who will bring a new energy, new enthusiasm, new blood, and new contacts and friends into your business.

> It's easier to promote standards of excellence when you treat employees as members of a professional team instead of a collection of crazy relatives at a holiday dinner party.

## The Secret of Hiring the Right People: Attitude over Experience

Kervin's employee problems began with his inability to identify and hire the right people. If your business, like Kervin's, has "improper personalities," make no mistake, it is because of management or owner shortfalls, not market conditions or lack of a talent pool. The right people are out there—you're just failing to recognize them.

This is where "human resource professionals" get mad at me.

Managers and owners too often hire people based on the wrong criteria, especially in the hospitality business. Pick any big hotel chain and look at its HR manual. It's as thick as a telephone book because employment professionals get paid for producing legal documents. They justify their existence, while simultaneously trying to mitigate liability by focusing on the fallback hiring position of "experience necessary." As far as helping pinpoint the right people to hire, these manuals are useless.

The problem with traditional approaches to human resources is that they place too much importance upon industry familiarity and too little on identifying the personality traits necessary to really drive customer reactions. When I ask bar and restaurant owners or managers if they have employees who are negative, unenergetic, or otherwise detrimental to the growth of the business, almost all of them say yes. These employees (you know who they are) are a cancer in your business — and it comes from their personalities. I cannot let cancers get in the business, and if one gets in, it has to be removed before it spreads. As soon as I sense someone is going to pull other employees down, they are gone.

Negative or cynical people, like some of those employees at Weber's, revert to feral behavior when placed in highly social settings like bars. Out-of-control, negligent employees don't create profitable customer reactions. Boring, low-energy employees, even if knowledgeable, aren't good at creating great reactions either. They may have "experience," but dull people can and do "infect" new, enthusiastic employees and suck the energy out of important initiatives.

Experience is not a factor in creating great customer reactions. Some of Kervin's worst and most dishonest employees had both experience *and* professional training! Many of the best ones had determination, principles, and optimism but little history in the bar business. I define employee greatness and potential for success in terms of attitude and energy, and we rarely interview for these qualities. Learning how to be a top-notch salesperson, server, bartender, customer service representative, host, security person, or front desk representative is not rocket science. In almost all cases, a smart, eager, communicative, sincere, and *willing* person can be taught to do any of these jobs in a matter of days.

Choosing new staff is an opportunity to make huge changes in the personality and efficiency of your business, the quality of service it provides, and the experience of your customers. You can teach well-selected employees the procedural skills necessary to make them successful. But you can't change someone's personal interaction skills . . . it will never happen. My four-step hiring process worked for Weber's, Angry Ham's, and every bar or restaurant where I've been involved in recruitment and training—and they are steps that will work for your business too: (1) identify your employee adjectives, (2) recruit through proper advertising, (3) identify winning personalities, and (4) select your winners.

### *Step One: Identify Your Employee Adjectives*

When you think of your favorite employees in the past, what comes to mind? A procedural element such as an organized workstation, neat paperwork, or promptness? No. What makes an employee memorable is her attitude and smile, the way she takes the time to make sure a customer is happy, the extra mile she goes to ensure orders are fulfilled and problems are solved. Her intrinsic qualities—her energy, sense of humor, eagerness, and contributions to the team—are the qualities you remember.

Rather than relying on job descriptions that simply quantify various positions' duties and correlating them with matching experience as a tool for identifying and hiring great employees, I use a more holistic approach. The first step in the process is selecting eight adjectives that best define the personality ideal for each job or role in your business. This is a critical step: it gives you new visions and goals for your own management objectives, new ways to measure employee success, and new ways to assess the performance of your own business.

Create a "Job Candidate Profile" for every job position in your business. Each Job Candidate Profile should contain eight single- and multiple-word phrases of defining adjectives that clearly describe the perfect employee for each job position. Consider employee-to-customer personality traits, colleague-to-colleague traits, and employee-to-manager traits when making up the list. For example, an accounting manager might be described with adjectives such as "accurate," "patient," "detailed," and "consistent." A cocktail server for a nightclub or casual restaurant would likely be described with adjectives like "energetic," "fun," "music-loving," "sports-loving," "good-humored," "sociable conversationalist," "adventurous," and so on. Obviously, the adjectives for front-of-house staff and back-of-house staff (normally unseen by guests) will be quite different.

Below is one generic example of a Job Candidate Profile. Your lists should be tailored for your particular bar concept, audience, location, and style of business (high-end, casual, neighborhood, tourist, and so on).

**BARTENDER**

1. Energetic
2. Extroverted/Conversational
3. Very Likable (first impression)
4. Hospitable, demonstrates a Great Service Attitude
5. Sports Loving
6. Cooperative, Team Player
7. Quality Orientated
8. Attentive, Good Listening Skills

**SAMPLE ADJECTIVES**

Amazing
Ambitious
Appealing
Ardent
Astounding
Avid
Awesome
Buoyant
Committed
Courageous
Creative
Dazzling
Dedicated
Delightful
Distinctive
Diverse
Dynamic
Eager

Energetic
Engaging
Entertaining
Enthusiastic
Entrepreneurial
Exceptional
Exciting
Fervent
Flexible
Friendly
Genuine
High-Energy
Imaginative
Impressive
Independent
Ingenious
Keen
Lively
Magnificent
Motivating
Outstanding
Passionate
Positive
Proactive
Remarkable
Resourceful
Responsive
Spirited
Supportive

Upbeat
Vibrant
Warm
Zealous

*Step Two: Recruit through Proper Advertising*

The next step is to develop print or online advertising copy that will attract the personalities you've just defined. The adjective description comes in handy now because there is nothing as ineffective as an ad that reads: "Bartender needed. Experience necessary." Laugh if you want, but I can't tell you how many times I see ads like this, even from big brands and high-end establishments — businesses that should know better. Employee adjectives incorporated into ad copy attracts candidates who naturally gravitate and respond positively to those adjectives and discourages those who don't.

For example, a quiet, shy, and low-confidence person won't respond to an ad that uses adjectives like "high-energy," "dynamic," and "fun-loving." Try to work at least five of your eight adjectives into your copy. Someone who feels he fits the description will be eager to respond to a job if it "sounds like me." Don't understate your case in an ad. Be assertive. Here are a few examples of ads that are proven winners, with the key adjectives bolded to demonstrate ways these words can be woven in:

GREAT JOBS ARE HARD TO FIND!
Not anymore! We are seeking a **fun, high-energy, customer-oriented** [insert the position you are looking to fill, i.e., server, bartender, hostess] for [insert your business name]. Our management

team is **dynamic** and **friendly,** with a **passion** for entertaining and great food! Apply in person [insert time(s)] on [insert day(s)] at [insert your address — include landmarks that make you easy to find]. [insert any benefits you offer]. EOE [equal opportunity employer]

ARE YOU LOOKING FOR A DIFFERENT KIND OF JOB?
We're a different kind of company seeking someone who is **passionate** about their job. The ideal person is **high-energy, extroverted,** and lives, breathes, and eats **enthusiastically!** Ours is a unique operation that you will be both challenged by and enjoy at the same time. If this sounds like you, get in touch with us soon . . . we're waiting to hear from you. Apply in person [insert time(s)] on [insert day(s)] at [insert your address — include landmarks that make you easy to find]. [insert any benefits you offer]. EOE [equal opportunity employer]

SEEKING **HIGH-ENERGY** PEOPLE . . . ARE YOU ONE?
Do you have a **warm, upbeat, positive** personality and a well-developed **sense of humor?** We're looking for people with the following skills, abilities, and experience: a love of service, a **keen** commitment to delighting the customer, a strong and **genuine** sense of integrity toward work and life, **independent** and **original** thinking, and **supportive** of others. We believe in work/life balance and recruiting people like ourselves. Apply in person [insert time(s)] on [insert day(s)] at [insert your address — include landmarks that make you easy to find]. [insert any benefits you offer]. EOE [equal opportunity employer]

Make it clear that applying is simple and convenient. Don't ask people to fax or send résumés in advance, or to call to make an appointment. Why do you want to sort through pieces of paper that tell you nothing about a person's personality? It's an extra step that most jobs in the bar or hospitality industry don't need to take. Unless you are filling a professional position that demands specific experience and knowledge, this strategy is a waste of everyone's time. Fielding phone calls and sifting through e-mails is just as tiresome. Extra steps also reduce the number of candidates who come in for an interview . . . and you want as many as possible. Instead, list afternoon and evening hours when you will be available to meet and interview prospective employees. Think of this adventure as a casting call — because it is. An open-door strategy also increases the number of people you can meet in a short amount of time, which improves your chances of finding great, dynamic candidates.

When filling high-level positions, I argue that personality, disposition, and point of view are more important than finding someone with industry-specific skills and experience. You owe it to yourself and your business to be open-minded. You may find someone from another industry who brings a new perspective, excitement, and energy to a high-level job. When Nightclub and Bar (NCB), owned by Questex Media Group, was struggling, president and CEO Kerry Gumas looked outside the trade show and media industry and focused on who the organization served — people actually in the restaurant and bar business. That led Gumas to me, and I accepted the position of president of the NCB, overseeing its trade show (the largest in the industry) and publications. I had never worked in trade shows or publishing, but a knowledgeable staff shortened my learning curve. Since taking over, revenue growth has been in the double digits, and I've launched two new events: VIBE (Very Important Beverage Executives) and the Hospitality Sports Marketing Conference.

*Step Three: Identify Winning Personalities*

The conventional interview process is bullshit. It focuses on experience only and not on personal dynamics. Candidates know the "right" answers to the questions they're asked. Useless. If I want to find someone who embodies the characteristics I've defined, I need to learn more about them than the canned answers to "What's your greatest weakness?" or "What did you like best about working at Denny's?" I use three *C*'s — Conversation, Conviction, and Curiosity — to find out what I need to know to judge if a candidate's personality meets up with my adjectives. I have a Conversation by asking questions that require expressive answers; I demonstrate Conviction about my company and the job I am offering to gauge if his passion matches mind; and I show Curiosity about the other person using "and" and "really."

For example: "Oh, you coach a traveling hockey team? Really?" or "Oh, in your free time you hit new restaurants? I love it . . . and?" Remember, any answer that indicates an intelligent interest and curiosity is a positive sign! During interviews, my list of adjectives is in front of me, and I put a check next to every word the candidate demonstrates as he talks. I can check off "foodie" next to the person who likes trying new restaurants and "competitive" on the sports coach's list. You want to know: Does this person have the disposition, physical capacity, and emotional intelligence to do X, Y, or Z? If you check off four or fewer adjectives on the list, his personality is wrong, so his experience is irrelevant. Next.

If a person's personality and interpersonal skills seem right, then (and only then) does his past experience become relevant to the discussion. Ask about his previous jobs, the skills he used, the special knowledge he has, and his vision of the job. How would he do it if given the opportunity? If he held a similar job in the past, how did he solve problems? Ask for specific examples. What strategies did he use with difficult employees or customers? If his work experience is limited but his personality is a good fit, find out as much as you can about how any past personal or school experiences could translate to the job. And if you are talking to a person who may be very experienced in another industry—the economy today has required many people to enter the hospitality field who bring a variety of professional skills to the table—ask how he feels his current skill set applies to the job. You may find that a candidate with the right personality but less direct experience is more "qualified" than a veteran of the business.

While you're talking, be sure to make note of body language and eye contact. If a candidate hesitates to look you in the eyes when he talks to you, that's a problem. If a candidate doesn't fully engage with you by leaning forward, relaxing, using hand gestures, or generally physically demonstrating an "outer directedness," he may not be a good fit for jobs that entail customer contact. Slow and soft talking, or quick and loud talking—these traits are difficult to change. Does the candidate's expressive style match what you're looking for?

Don't forget to identify potential hires' buckets: money, ego, pride, or fear. The money conversation is easy: "You can increase your income by 200 percent and this is what you have to do to make that happen." Someone in the money bucket can go in a pressure cooker, the busiest shift, because people motivated by money will rise to whatever the occasion demands if there's profit in it. The ego-bucket person is motivated by an important-sounding title — which costs you nothing — or a chance to win an award for service or sales. People in the pride bucket can be put together on a shift because they'll try to one-up each other and, as a result, produce superior work. Schedule detail-oriented, risk-averse people — the fear bucket — during slower-paced shifts, like afternoons, commonly frequented by mature customers who expect patient and conscientious service.

### *Step Four: Select Your Winners*

Once the "auditions" are done, you have to decide which candidates best meet the criteria you've set for the job. The candidates who match up with at least six of the eight adjectives are hirable. Keep in mind that the most important function of your staff is to establish customer relationships and reflect the personality and profile of your business and brand. So you have to look carefully at the two missing adjectives and determine if they're deal breakers. For instance, if I have a sports bar and "sports-loving" and "fast-paced" aren't checked off, the person is probably not going to work. Will you compromise your standards and give in to convenience by hiring the person anyway? That decision is one of the most defining moments for a manager. You will do one of two things: fight for your standards and customers and not hire the person, or compromise all of that and offer him a job for the sake of convenience. Remember, selecting your new team is the biggest opportunity you have to impact your business.

## Teach, Don't Train

In the hospitality industry, the word "training" is very common, even though we don't train anybody. We only teach people to work in our business. Training is behavior modification; it takes too long. Teaching is showing someone how to carry out specific tasks and then encouraging them to add their personalities in to make their role come alive. I mean, you just spent a lot of time finding the right personalities for your bar. Why would you then ask these people to suppress the qualities that attracted you? Employees who express their unique personalities develop relationships with customers and therefore build customer satisfaction, guest frequency, and brand loyalty. The last thing you want is to dampen great personalities. Rather, you want personalities to emerge and become part of an employee's ability to serve, care for, and satisfy customers.

None of this means that standards do not apply — they do — but there is more than one good way to say hello, take and fill an order, and serve a drink. You might even learn something from your employees when you let them be themselves and contribute ideas. You will also have a happier work force — employees feel more connected and satisfied when they are not confined to rigid and repetitive structural procedures that muffle their natural interpersonal inclinations.

Teach the four dynamics to employees: personal, mechanical, interactive, and group. These principles provide a platform to define and use unique personal characteristics to everyone's benefit. It also increases employee understanding of *your* behavioral objectives.

**Personal Dynamics.** Encourage employees to present themselves in a dynamic and authentic way that allows their personalities to shine.

Let them show what they've got — they love food, let them talk about it. Sports fanatics in a sports bar? Go with it. When each person on a team feels comfortable being open, fun, and vibrant in his or her own distinctive way, customers feel more connected to the experience. It breaks down barriers between the guest and the worker and, therefore, between the guest and the brand or business. Role-play with employees if you have time — let them practice on each other as "guest" and "server" to build their confidence.

**Mechanical Dynamics.** Teach workers the mechanics of service that fit your bar concept or brand. If delivery is too slow, it robs energy from the experience (and pisses people off). If it's too fast, it robs customers of their perceived value (and makes customers feel as if they're being rushed). The mechanics of a job greatly affects customer impressions of the business — and those mechanics must match the kind of place you're operating. For example: Denny's is an inexpensive diner with bright lights and fast-moving servers — the T-bone steak is one of the most expensive items on the menu and it's less than $20. Per Se, one of the most expensive restaurants in New York City, features soft lighting and elegant, slower-moving servers. In theory, if the lights were as bright and the servers as fast as they are at Denny's, Per Se would lose some of its allure and would no longer be able to charge $295 for its tasting menu. Discuss the key movements, serving style, and mechanical objectives that help connect the ambiance and offerings of your business with customer expectations. With consistent follow-up to instill and maintain a high standard of dynamic behavior, your staff will see what a difference it makes to their bottom line and their enjoyment of the job. These are the kinds of employee incentives that help your business.

**Interactive Dynamics.** In my bars, customers are more likable, better looking, and better dressed. They wear nicer watches and more fabulous shoes. That's because my employees make my guests feel smarter, funnier, and cooler than they do in any other bar in the neighborhood. There's a major theme park where the greeter will pick up the homeliest child and tell her mother, "She's so adorable!" The only other person who does that is the kid's grandmother. That one interactive dynamic makes that mother's day and—let me tell you—she has a great time with her daughter at that theme park. Encourage employees to interact with customers in a dynamic way. It's perfectly okay, even in high-end establishments, for servers or waitstaff to compliment customers on their attire, ask them how they are, and make small talk as long as it is unobtrusive and professional and reflects the feeling your establishment is trying to create. In a fine dining restaurant, for example, a waiter wouldn't talk about sports scores with diners during a business lunch or dinner unless the diner brings it up first. But it's perfectly acceptable to say hello, ask after guests, and proactively discuss the menu. The waiter can "up-sell" without being pushy or obnoxious, and establishes trust in the process. Customers ask for certain waiters precisely because their service, recommendations, and knowledge of the food are so excellent. Again, let the staff role-play. It loosens everyone up and it's a great way for employees to hone their techniques.

**Group Dynamics.** Every individual who works for you works for the team (remember the warning I gave you about managing staff like a family). Reinforce the team message constantly; a shared identity creates unity and a motivated staff. Back to front, top to bottom, every staff member must be on the same page, understand what you're trying to achieve, and work in unison to create the reactions that meet the objectives of the business. Promote collegiality among colleagues through active communication. Begin each shift with a brief staff meeting to review anticipated guest count, special events, VIP guests expected to come, and the role each employee will play in making the evening a success. These meetings should be as inclusive as possible — that means your dish machine operator (DMO) and busboys are just as important to the process as the general manager and hostess.

Minimize the differences among various levels of employees; instead, focus on the fact that everyone makes an important contribution *because it's true.* For instance, I never use the term "dishwasher." DMO elevates the job in everyone's mind and expresses the importance of having clean dishes and glassware. Anything I can do to promote pride in an employee's work is a good manipulation. Insist on mutually respectful behavior from those who are charged with managing work assignments and directing workers during busy times or staff shortages. As an owner or manager, you should talk and actively listen to everyone.

You also have to accept that people are idiosyncratic, with funny habits that are revealed as time goes on and workers settle into their jobs. Notice these habits with strategic objectivity, and figure out how to work with them if they are part of the "package" a winning employee brings to the table. I managed a successful chain of restaurants years ago, and in one location I had an absolutely terrific waiter. "Dave" was never late for a shift and was cheerfully willing to fill in when others were absent, and he had fabulous personal dynamics, effortlessly up-selling the menu. He had a following of loyal customers who loved to come to the restaurant in part just to sit in

Dave's section. Dave made me money—and he made phenomenal tips. The only problem was that his station was a mess. Dave did not follow protocol when it came to maintaining the neatness and order of his area. It drove a few of his fellow waiters crazy, and my assistant manager was in a constant state of annoyance because of the chaos at workstation number three.

Traditional restaurant management wisdom suggests that Dave should have been written up for a messy station or verbally corrected. The result of this typical approach leaves an otherwise brilliant employee (loved by customers) and a dependable high sales performer feeling unappreciated, criticized, and possibly angered. If you do something to make an employee like Dave walk out the door, who's the idiot then? It would be better to figure out a way to minimize his weakness.

To guide Dave toward improvement while still maintaining his enthusiasm and motivation, I used personal reinforcement with professional correction.

"Dave, you're one of my favorite employees," I said. "Our customers love you, the staff loves you, your sales are always great, and I can always count on you. I'm really proud you're here . . . very proud. But we [never 'I'] have one issue to work out. We need to find a way to get your station cleaner at the end of the night. What do you think—what could we do to help you do that? Because, buddy, this place is a heck of a mess!" We laughed, but Dave got the message without feeling dismissed or misunderstood. Together we worked out a game plan that broke cleaning up into stages throughout his shift. This change was so subtle, few employees even noticed the difference. The only change they did notice was that Dave's station looked a lot better.

Every time you communicate with an employee, the interaction must end with the employee being more motivated, more eager, and more likely to perform better — this is a critical objective. A positive but honest approach keeps the work atmosphere fun and functioning. When you notice employees doing something right, say something. "That was dynamic, Jenny," or "Great customer dynamics, George," or "John, that was a fantastic save — good problem solving — I'm going to share what you did at the next staff meeting." That way, employees will be much more open and responsive when you have to tell them, "You had a chance to be more dynamic," or "You could have handled that situation differently, and here's how."

### A COOK'S TALE

Most bars need to hire at least one cook, maybe two, depending on your service hours and concept. There are thousands of chefs in America who have been professionally trained, have mentored with great chefs, and have spent years mastering their craft. This is why I hate it when a cook calls himself a chef. A cook is a cook and a chef is a chef. If someone does not have educational credentials or at least fifteen years of experience in great venues, he is not a chef. Most bars can get along very well with a competent, trained cook who may have training and experience, so for the majority of bars a professional chef is an unnecessary and costly extra. However, a cook should still be able to turn out consistently tasty, well-plated food; maintain kitchen standards including cleanliness; and ensure that inventory is fresh.

Cooks and chefs are a commodity, no different from lawyers or accountants. That means you can pick and choose the cook who can fulfill your needs precisely. If you want to open an Irish pub, hire someone who knows Irish food. American food? Hire someone who knows classic American bar fare. You can get a real pizza guy to do pizza if a pizza oven is the centerpiece of your food program and bar concept. This is so much better than hiring a cook (or chef) who claims to do it all. A generic cook will often produce generic food.

Finally, do not be intimidated by the cook. Cooks have a reputation for being emotional, domineering, and bossy. But the cook works for you; you hire him and manage him — he does not manage you. You provide the vision and he executes it. The cook has to understand your costs and standards, and those things come directly from you, not from the cook. Once all of that is understood, you can allow him to create great plates of food within that envelope. If you do not have the confidence to manage your cook or chef and he ends up managing you, it is only a matter of time before the kitchen holds you hostage.

## Set Standards and Commit to Them

I believe management has to fight to maintain standards every day. If a standard is not qualifiable (what you are supposed to do), quantifiable (when or how often you are supposed to do it), and verifiable (management can check to make sure it was done), it is not a standard. What are yours? And how are you communicating them? If employees don't know what you want and expect, they aren't going to deliver. I'll say it again: If standards are not being met, do not blame your employees or the economy. Blame management.

Keep in mind that you're setting priorities for employees all the time . . . even when you don't know it. I determine where their eyes go and how they spend their time when the bar isn't busy. If I make a habit of noticing when lightbulbs are out, my staff will look up all the time; if I mention the condition of the floors on a regular basis, they will look down. In other words, what's important to me becomes important to them — so I choose wisely and consciously what I focus on. If you remind employees to keep the floors clean many times throughout the day, the floors will be clean because you've set a priority for floor cleanliness. If a manager says, "Don't worry about the floors, guys," naturally the floors are not going to be as clean. So, to effect a new, dynamic approach to service, you need to establish what is important and convey it to your staff. Manage and meet standards by example. Walk the walk. Be as dynamic as you want your employees to be. Show them that you can take out the trash and wipe off a table with the best of them.

# 5

# Four-Walls Marketing

> The aim of marketing is to know and understand the customer so well that the product or service fits him and sells itself.
>
> — PETER F. DRUCKER, MANAGEMENT CONSULTANT, *THE ESSENTIAL DRUCKER*

WHEN MY WIFE, NICOLE, and her girlfriend Valerie met at Swanky Bubbles in downtown Philadelphia, they were eager to get a firsthand look at why the bar had hit the skids in the last few years. The cocktail lounge opened in 1999 on a trend — champagne — that enabled it to thrive for a while. The trouble with fads is their ephemeral nature, in one day and out the next. Cigar bars came and went very quickly despite smoking laws. Put an of-the-moment item on a menu — it's pretty low risk. If it doesn't sell, or when the moment passes, you can quickly replace it with something else. Basing a business on a very specific trend embraces an unacceptable amount of risk. In this case, the very nature of the concept left them behind.

There were other packaging errors at Swanky Bubbles beyond the silly name and outdated concept. Nicole and Valerie were handed a big one as soon as they sat down.

"I could have bench-pressed the food and drink menus," Nicole observed. "That's how humungous they were." It was true — the oversized cocktail and food offerings were bound in physically heavy and bulky material, and the narrow pages of myriad offerings were overwhelming and oddly varied.

Entrées ran the gamut from sushi and mac and cheese, to gnocchi and nachos. Not only that, but everything was printed in a thick black typeface, with no visual differentiation between appetizers and entrées. Pages and pages of minimally categorized dishes served to confuse rather than entice. The drink list was no better — there were so many strangely named, multi-ingredient cocktails that the bar manager couldn't keep the required spirits on hand to make them.

"Why would anyone want something called Romeo and Juliet's Love Elixir?" Nicole asked the bartender. "Wasn't that arsenic?" No matter, the bar didn't have the ingredients to make it even if someone did want to gamble on her life and order it. Nor was there vanilla cognac, the defining ingredient of a drink Nicole and Valerie *did* want to try. This was an unintended advantage, since the bartender admitted to my wife and her friend that it was a terrible drink.

Co-owner Ryan Dorsey checked in with the ladies to see what was wrong, and when Nicole expressed her disappointment at the lack of vanilla cognac, he comped both women a cocktail each. Nicole was persuaded to try the Sexual Chocolate Martini, which Dorsey said would be him, "if I was a cocktail." After taking psychological hot showers to wash away Ryan's gross and inappropriate behavior, Nicole and Valerie finished their drinks and left early. Ego, the belief that you're a big shot because you own a bar, leads to various destructive behaviors, including blindness to marketing problems, giving profits away through customer freebies, and taking advantage of your imaginary and inflated position by propositioning guests.

The way we communicate today is constant, instantaneous, and manifold—traditional advertising isn't nearly as memorable as it once was. People remember experiences—good and bad. No one remembers average. Nicole and Valerie will never forget their Swanky Bubbles experience. It communicated all the wrong messages, starting with the bar's ridiculous name and burdensome menus, and ending with service that was a complete turnoff. Since the ladies' experience was typical of that of most other female customers of the establishment, it was not difficult to understand why the bar's guest traffic and revenues had gone flat.

Bars sell reactions and generate revenue by packaging cohesive narratives through various physical and experiential attributes that reinforce a bar's purpose—the concept, name, menu appearance, cocktail offerings, and frequency marketing. Owners often pass over this critical marketing method—even though it guarantees results—and instead move directly to conventional, expensive, and unpredictable external advertising programs, promotions, and discounting to drive business. My goal is to change the way you market by teaching you the value of "four-walls marketing."

T.G.I. Friday's was the first bar that truly understood and optimized four-walls marketing. Manhattan perfume salesman Alan Stillman opened the first T.G.I. Friday's in 1965 at First Avenue and Sixty-Third Street, then a burgeoning hub of young, professional singles. He wanted to find a way to get models and flight attendants out of their walk-up studio apartments and into a social space where he could meet them and mingle. Those were the days when a single working guy could still afford to buy a broken-down beer joint in Manhattan, which is exactly what Stillman did. He added personality with wooden floors, Tiffany-style lamps, bentwood chairs, striped tablecloths, and authentic and unique memorabilia. It was like no other place on the block—or the city.

It didn't take long for Stillman's flight attendant fantasy to come true—pretty girls from all over the city flocked to the bar, and with them came young men. After a week, New York City police officers had to control the massive line of eager revelers that snaked around the block. Just a decade later there were ten Friday's restaurants in eight states, and today the company franchises and licenses more than a thousand bar-restaurants in sixty-one countries and continues to expand its reach into new global markets. Until quite recently, Stillman, and the subsequent owners of the restaurant, based the chain's success strictly on the technique of four-walls marketing—unlike Chili's and other similar casual dining venues, Friday's did no expensive advertising.

Four-walls marketing means marketing from the inside out, creating such a distinctive, powerful, and memorable experience that people want to return, bring their friends, and talk up the place with neighbors and colleagues. T.G.I. Friday's is synonymous with flair bartending, a focus on interesting cocktails, and a sense of energy and fun. Although it has changed its décor with the times, every element of Friday's is unified and reinforces its story—from signage and menus to plating and service. It's clearly the most successful chain of bar-oriented casual restaurants in the country, if not the world. To me, Friday's sets the standard for the category. In the interest of full disclosure, I'm proud to consult for Friday's and I have the highest respect for the brand — and have since I went to my first Friday's as a kid growing up in New York.

Four-walls marketing includes building appearance, signage, décor, furniture, music, lighting, space planning, and flow. I talk about these components in subsequent chapters. The focus here is on the aspects of packaging that are often overlooked or implemented without due consideration — your business's name, menu, featured items, signature dishes, special promotions, servers' appearance, and plating strategies. Every one of these elements, properly executed, sells reactions and significantly increases revenue beyond the bottom line. For instance, strategic menu design leads customers to make profitable decisions; promotional efforts transform an infrequent drop-in to a regular who brings her friends along for a good time; thoughtful plating creates enthusiasm that builds repeat business.

> Bars need to be conceived and built for the local audience, not the personal tastes of the owner.

## Who's Reacting?

Before you make naming, drink and food, and menu design decisions, you need to understand who your customers are demographically, where they live, and how they spend their money. It is easier, less expensive, and more profitable to fit a business into a particular location rather than force a location to fit a business. When a bar entrepreneur tells me he's going to "educate" the market, I write him off. Sure, you can educate consumers about certain products, but a bar is not one of them. Most bars serve markets and existing interests. If you already own several successful bars and have money to burn, go ahead and experiment with educating a market. See how it goes. You might get lucky. If you want to invest in a single bar and are a first-time owner, play it safe and let the market educate you.

In other words, a singles bar in an area populated mostly by married people with young children isn't going to work. Married people have no reason to be seen in such a place, and if they do, the singles bar in the next town seems like a safer bet. Singles are not going to travel outside their comfort zone for a drink and a hookup. A biker bar and poolroom will languish in an area comprising mainly a suit-and-tie lunch crowd. Neighborhood or demographic analysis is crucial in figuring out who the likely audience is in a particular geographic area. Unfortunately, not enough entrepreneurs bother studying the market before deciding on a concept.

Research mitigates risk—doing my homework has made me successful for more than thirty-five years. It is incredibly unreasonable to suggest that I innately know what a marketplace wants. That's absurd. Markets express and identify trends and taste. Your ideas, like mine, should come from a desire to fill an underserved need or desire in an existing market. Sometimes these "pockets of need" are visible. For instance, say you're walking around the Geary Boulevard District in San Francisco and you notice there are no fast-food chains in sight. "Hmm . . . ," you think. "Maybe this is a great opportunity to open a Subway or a burger franchise." Not so fast. Never make an assumption (let alone a business decision) based on the absence of something. Do your homework. It turns out that in 1987 the San Francisco City Council used zoning laws to restrict large fast-food restaurants from opening in the district. It was over turned in 2011, but despite this, a big chain would still face hostility from its potential neighbors. The real solution might be to open an independent sandwich and grill bar with a quick and casual concept.

To succeed, you have to discern whether people really want food fast (as opposed to fast food). If so, what location in the area has the most potential to reach customers, and what elements of your business would attract the market? You need a great deal of information to answer these questions. If you don't get the information, your budget is a fantasy, which means *you* are in fantasyland, period, end of discussion. Unfortunately, a lot of would-be owners stop before they get the answers — they see what looks like a golden opportunity and act on it without doing more legwork. In these situations, I can tell you that the majority of the time, the projections they make are inaccurate and overly optimistic.

Gathering statistics, demographic research, and the knowledge gleaned from old-fashioned footwork is the only way to uncover what the market is saying. It's futile and too risky to go into any brick-and-mortar consumer business without a thorough investigation. When I open a bar or any business, I define the appropriate geographic market area, which could be a few blocks in Manhattan or a stretch of miles in California. I get a map and a Magic Marker and draw a polygon or a circle that represents this area. I compile a list of all the towns near my intended spot and gather general credit card data on those towns, discarding neighborhoods that generate the lowest numbers. Once I define an approximate area, I buy detailed personal and economic reports and begin painting a picture of the existing customer base.

This data includes income averages; how many people are married and how many are single; how old they are; how many children they have, including average ages; what kind of education they have; how residents spend money on food, liquor, entertainment, and travel; and how many times during a week people dine out versus dine in. I can also buy data on how many other bars and restaurants are in the area, how many grocery stores and shopping malls are nearby, and how many and what kinds of small business, schools, gyms, doctors, and hospitals exist in my radius. Customer charge card receipts, organized by locality, enable me to calculate sales volume generated by specific areas during specific times.

Much of this information is available from the Census Bureau and various state sources for free (e.g., county planning boards). Reference books such as *The Sourcebook of Zip Code Demographics*, published annually by CACI Inc., includes demographic and economic information on neighborhoods. We live in the information age, and there are many companies that collect and sort all kinds of economic and social data—and sell it. You name it—there's a report on it. These reports are affordable (from $30 to $500, depending on the detail of information you want) and arrive on your computer in seconds.

*Bar Rescue* uses Esri (esri.com), a geographic information system (GIS) and mapping software that provides location analysis, to look at buying habits within specific population clusters. Some mapping companies document regional malls, shopping centers larger than one hundred thousand square feet, and major highways and roads in any selected area, and then pinpoints potential customers through patterns and colors that represent estimated median household income ranging from $0 to $112,000 per year. Mapping reports also show population density or number of households in specific locations. Donnelley Marketing Information Services can map extremely finite areas, from a one- to five-mile radius from specific city intersections, to plot expenditure and shopping center locations. These kinds of services map population shifts and ethnic clusters in major cities. The point is, no matter which of these sources you use, find out who is in your market and what they want. Otherwise, how can you build a product for them that will be successful for you?

Once I have the necessary research in hand, I dissect it to figure out where my desired customers are most heavily clustered. If you can't understand a report, the good news is that all mapping and data analysis companies provide help lines with people ready to walk you through the findings. My work isn't done quite yet. The next thing I do is get in my car. There is a great deal to learn about a location just by driving around and scrutinizing what you see. It's called fieldwork — think of yourself as a cultural anthropologist on a mission to discover how the natives live. A keen and sensitive observer can collect valuable material simply by being fully present and aware — and then connecting the dots of what you learn.

I look at the businesses that seem to be thriving, the décor and design of these businesses, the kinds of cars parked nearby — shitty pickups (blue-collar workers) or brand-new, tricked-out trucks ("gentleman farmer" types)? Do recently issued minivans and SUVs predominate (families, soccer moms) or are there a lot of two-seater, ego, sports cars and hybrids around (singles, young marrieds)? Are four-door sedans and town cars a common sight (older empty nesters)?

How do people on the street dress? What does the lunch crowd in the local restaurants look like — young mothers, businessmen, or babysitters and nannies with kids? How about dinnertime — do most of the restaurants cater to couples or families? Are the bars filled with sports lovers or young singles? Do the people dress up or are they very casual? Look for cultural shifts in neighborhoods. Are houses being renovated? Are salons and spas opening or closing? Are health clubs and spinning studios sprouting up in place of day care centers? Have big-box stores arrived in town or is a more bustling downtown shopping scene erupting?

Now I can home in on the makeup, habits, and "flavor" of the market. Over several weeks, I begin to fill in the picture with more details; I see what's working in the area and how key economic indicators are changing and what they mean. Suddenly it hits me between the eyes, and the neighborhood and its needs and wants start to make sense. Now I can identify three key factors for my bar: the right concept (cocktails, sports bar, etc.); the right delivery system (sophisticated, casual, etc.); and the most promising locations.

## Be Clear on Concept

Once your demographic becomes clear, you can pinpoint the concept that makes the most sense. If your bar intends to serve food—and most bars do serve some kind of edible product—its food program must be driven by logic. The first step to maximize food sales in a bar is to understand its purpose. There are four basic food program styles that a bar can successfully pull off—and in order to get all your messaging and four-walls marketing right, you have to figure out what your style is before you develop a food program, let alone open or rebrand your business. I take a piece of paper and make a list of the variables that help me determine the food program that would work best for my bar. How big is the kitchen and what can it produce and still maintain quality? Are people mainly drinking and see food as something quick to sustain them through the evening? What's my price point for food? What's my revenue potential in the market with tiny tapas? Or "gourmet" sandwiches or grilled wraps? Comfort food or lighter fare?

At Swanky Bubbles, the owners tried to revamp the tired champagne theme through a food program. The result was a haphazard mess. Mac and cheese and sushi on the same menu is wrong on so many levels. Was it a casual comfort food bar or a late-night, sophisticated light-bite kind of place? Moreover, would you really trust the level and quality of sushi fish in a place that also rolled out crocks of pasta covered in orange cheese? If you'll recall from chapter one, the food program at Downey's, a famous Irish pub, became muddled when owner/chef Domenic Centofanti added Italian dishes to the lineup. Food programs that suffer from an identity crisis confuse guests and drive them away.

Within the four food programs that work best in a bar, there is a tremendous amount of leeway in terms of the exact dishes you offer.

**Convenience Dining.** Quick, inexpensively priced food that is prepared as a convenience to guests while they are drinking and partying. Your menu, products, and pricing must fit into this logic by being quick and easy to prepare, and priced to sell, meaning inexpensive. If patrons' stomachs start to growl and they want to add some sustenance so they can keep drinking, an upscale bar might offer exotic mixed olives, roasted herbed walnuts, and curried chicken bites, while a more casual place could present mini hot dogs, chicken wings, small spring rolls, potato skins, or jalapeño poppers. The variety demonstrates that you can go in several food directions and still achieve convenience dining. Table service (waiters and waitresses) isn't typically necessary for grab-and-eat-style dishes. An extensive or large kitchen isn't required to turn out a high-quality product either—so it's a perfect solution for a location that's small and wants to focus on beverage service. The food comes right out of the kitchen in its serving vessel, from which the food is also consumed. Napkins and toothpicks are a must, but utensils are often unnecessary.

**Cooperative Bar Dining.** This program provides food that "co-operates" with a bar's or nightclub's experience and is well suited to laid-back lounge-style venues. The food is sold and eaten at the bar, as above, but offerings are more extensive and more "meal-like" than convenience dining, which is essentially small bites—finger or cocktail food. Let me clarify further by saying this is not the same as having dinner at the bar à la Morton's or similar restaurants where the bartender will place an entire table setup in front of you, complete with place mat, napkins, silverware, water glass, and bread basket. In these situations, the food is created to deliberately interact with the liquor experience. At the Hawthorne in Boston, the bar and kitchen work in unison to create imaginative pairings between cocktails and small bites. The food program survives only if guests, who initially came by for a drink, are inspired to order food spontaneously; otherwise you'll fail every time. At the Bamboo Beach Club and Tiki Bar, right on the water in Fort Lauderdale, Florida, the menu went from fried and disgusting to fresh and enticing during its *Bar Rescue* makeover. It now includes casual and local items that are in sync with its specialty cocktails and its surroundings: salads, fish, various sandwiches, and lobster. Table service is minimal since the tables are located in the bar area and the establishment does not have a separate dining room. A basic kitchen setup is all that's required to turn out the kind of simple but fresh fare at Bamboo.

**Interactive Dining.** This food program requires a separate environment and experience that appeals to couples or groups who want a quieter, more intimate, and less energetic sit-down "break" from the din of a higher-energy bar or nightclub. In this case, the environment is the initial attraction. That means the music, service, lighting, and other aspects of the room reinforce a subdued feeling. Food and environment must mesh because frequency is driven by the quality and experience of the combination. Servers take orders as they do in a traditional restaurant. You can serve more unexpected and original dishes in this kind of bar.

**Signature Dining.** This bar's objective is to give patrons a unique culinary experience. Examples include a prime steak house, a sushi or raw bar, and even a handcrafted, artisanal pizza restaurant. A guest's decision to visit this operation is based upon curiosity, a desire to try the food. Like interactive dining, a signature dining objective requires a separate dining room, wait service, and creative, thoughtful attention to dining experience details, such as more unique plating techniques and tabletop details. The Alembic Bar in San Francisco, one of *Food & Wine*'s top fifty American bars, is a "gastropub" — it takes both its local food and its "craft" cocktails and libations equally seriously, making it a natural for the signature dining category. Pickled quail eggs, jerk spiced duck hearts, Peking duck breast, and bone marrow — this is high-end dining at a high-end bar.

## What's in a Name? Money.

Naming is an integral part of both reassessments of an existing brand and the formulation of a new business, never an afterthought. When consumers' perspectives on fried food and health changed, Kentucky Fried Chicken strategically renamed the brand KFC. It was a brilliant move that helped fight the negative association the general public had with fried foods — even though fried chicken sales still outpace grilled offerings at the company. The name change also blunted any growing concerns about animal rights, which had started to shift into the mainstream. Getting rid of the word "chicken" allowed the chain to offer a more varied menu and avoid public disapproval over the company's associations with inhumane livestock practices, which it had been linked to in the press. Losing the word "Kentucky" freed it from any off-putting regional associations.

With very few exceptions, I change the names of most bars I work with on *Bar Rescue.* Even a subtle tweak can help both the public and management see the place in a new way. It signals a fresh start, a new beginning, another chance for success. The Bamboo Beach Tiki Bar was altered slightly, to the Bamboo Beach Club and Tiki Bar. It was the best of both worlds in terms of the passersby and residents most prone to see the bar. Locals do not go to tiki bars because they are perceived as touristy, but they will go to a "beach club." Tourists are less inclined to go to a place designated solely as a "club" because the impression is that it's reserved for locals. The trouble with the original name was that it created the perception of the bar as a tourist trap that adjoined a hotel. The slight adjustment to the name, which seems so easy, had a great deal of thought behind it; the right change was crucial in getting both visitors and locals to the bar. The addition of "club" suggested that the al fresco waterfront venue was part of the community and not simply a tourist destination. We wanted more locals to stop by and recommend the place to visitors.

The Olive Pit (which I discuss further in chapter six) became the O.P. in our overall effort to modernize the Orange County, California, bar and eliminate the common joke among locals that the place was "a pit." The original name created a disconnect—when people heard "olive," they thought "martinis," and the bar didn't make martinis. The O.P. maintains the history and heritage of the place while freshening its image. It also plays off the nickname of its location, "the O.C." We changed the Mystique Lounge to Aura Nightclub because murder and mayhem was so closely associated with the urban venue's original name—it had been the site of a sensational killing. We had to erase that ugly chapter in the nightclub's past if we wanted to bring back its original upscale, youthful, and law-abiding clientele.

New names have to make sense from a marketing perspective—you don't paste a different label on a failing enterprise in the hopes of fooling people into thinking everything else has changed too.

Back to Swanky Bubbles: I couldn't make up a worse name if I tried, and it no longer had any relevance since the champagne craze had fallen by the wayside. The old name killed the joint because people reacted negatively to its somewhat creepy and old-fashioned vibe. It was retro, but not in a good way. What was trying to be cool and playful was, in reality, more like a frat boy's flat attempt at irony.

The new name had to connect to the strategy of our overhaul, which was to create a bar that women felt comfortable in, so comfortable that they would bring their friends for a girls' night out. The name Sheer fit with the strategy. It worked because it was simple, classic, and sexy without being overtly feminine. It fit with the other changes we made to the interior of the bar and to its menu and overall vibe. Women related to the name because it reminded them of stockings and lingerie. Men related to the name because . . . it reminded them of stockings and lingerie.

Sheer also didn't lock the owners into a trend — if champagne and bubbly cocktails ever came back into fashion, a bar named Sheer could certainly capitalize on the trend without becoming enslaved by it.

(Unbelievably, after we left the owners changed the name back to Swanky Bubbles, and predictably it failed to meet its revenue goals even though every other improvement we had made stayed in place. Not long after, it closed for good. What a shame.)

Switching or revising a name is one of the most difficult changes for an owner to accept, even if intellectually he realizes the name is part of what's holding back a bar's success. Overattachment to certain aspects of your business places you firmly in the social category of bar owner because the attachment has everything to do with emotions and little to do with strategy. I understand that a business is like a child — that's why people refer to bars and restaurants as "my baby" — so I get why renaming is a challenge. How often do people change the names of their sons and daughters? You have to stop thinking of your business as an extension of your gene pool.

The Canyon Inn in Yorba Linda, California, regularly fielded phone calls from travelers looking for an available room . . . which would have been great, had it been a hotel. But this sports bar and grill did not, in fact, have any rooms to let. I felt it was important to give the place a different and more accurate identity. The new name — Canyon Saloon Spirits and Steaks — made it clear to everyone exactly what the establishment specialized in. Unfortunately, co-owner Pauly Ambrus and his partner, like many owners I meet, were extremely attached to the original name of the bar and changed it back after I left. I urge you to consider whether your heart is overruling your head when it comes to your business name.

There are times when you should keep a name. If a business has a long history in a community and most of it is good and fondly remembered, there's no reason to throw those good feelings and memories away. This is why we chose not to change the name of the Abbey Pub in Chicago and Downey's in Philadelphia. Champs Sports Pub was Burbank's first and therefore oldest sports bar and for a long time a beloved institution — you shouldn't rewrite that kind of history. These were well-known and storied establishments, and we wanted to bring them back to their original glory. History is great — old and dated is bad.

When choosing a name, whether for a revamp of an old business or as the crowning glory of a new one, you have a tremendous opportunity to convey a lot of information in a concise and clever way. Don't blow it. The name must reflect what the bar wants to achieve. Ask a series of questions: What kind of service will you provide? What kind of audience do you want to attract? How does it fit within the neighborhood? Is it a place for professionals to meet? The Bull and Bear in the Waldorf Astoria in New York City has been welcoming the business crowd for decades, who can watch the stock ticker as they throw down a beer or a scotch on the rocks.

Are you specializing in certain kinds of drinks? The Martini Club in Munich, considered one of the world's best new contemporary bars, has a name that conjures up sophistication that the bar fulfills with its array of classic mixed drinks as well as innovative cocktails, knowledgeable bartenders, and intimate setting that makes patrons feel as if they are special guests in a private Prohibition-era lounge. Artisanal, a bustling bistro in Manhattan, offers more than a hundred wines by the glass and two hundred varieties of cheese. The name conveys the idea that individual, carefully chosen selections await guests.

Is the business located in a historical building or location? The French Laundry, in Napa Valley, California, is considered to be one of America's best restaurants—its name comes from the building it's in, which was once home to a nineteenth-century French steam laundry. Do you have a theme? The Beauty Bar, a successful chain of bars with locations in major cities across the country, began in an actual old beauty salon, and some still offer grooming services like manicures.

Do you want to join the tradition of great dive bars? Then you need a dive bar name—something that conveys flashing neon and old-school charm. The famed Frolic Room in Los Angeles fits the bill in name and ambiance. The carefully crafted shabby character of the bar's long, narrow space makes it impossible not to gab with your neighbors as you guzzle a short one or a beer fresh from the tap.

## Menu Magic—It's Science, Really

Menu engineering is the greatest single four-walls marketing opportunity for any bar or restaurant. It's also a huge opportunity for food operations in any setting. But few operators actually take advantage of it. Rather than steer guests toward more profitable items, most restaurants give the guest a free-for-all snapshot of offerings or, worse, unknowingly direct guest menu selections to their lower-revenue, less profitable items.

Another mistake too many bars and restaurants make is offering too many items. Small, simple menus have many benefits. First, visual simplicity is less confusing than an avalanche of choices. Big menus don't support the narrative most bars are trying to achieve—relaxation, socialization, and fun or romance. Forcing people to take up their valuable down time to read through a lengthy directory of dishes is inconsiderate. In fact, it adversely affects sales: guests are willing to spend about 109 seconds looking at a menu, after which they become fatigued and buy less.

Smaller menus have a significant revenue advantage. They sell more products, food costs are often lower, and inventory is easier to manage and maintain. A modest number of offerings allows your cook to focus on making each dish well. This does not mean you can't offer seasonal items or dishes that represent holidays or special occasions—please do. Specials add to the excitement and anticipation of repeat customers curious to know what you've cooked up next. Dishes made with seasonal ingredients take advantage of vendor deals. There is always a way to add new or temporary items to an elegantly concise menu so it needn't be boring.

How many items you have on the menu is driven by your concept—these decisions have to be made with the bar concept in mind. You may want to weigh the menu more toward appetizers and less so toward entrées. How do you want to weigh protein versus vegetarian dishes? Fish versus poultry? Weigh what foods best define your concept with what your kitchen can do and what your staff can accomplish. In general, most bar menus should be no longer than three pages or sections.

Lastly, people don't like to be presented with too many choices. I recall reading about a study about colored jellybeans. The researchers placed various bowls of the candy in a room separated by color—red, blue, pink, green, orange, yellow, black, and so on. They counted how many jellybeans were consumed and tallied up the totals. Some people took a few from two or three different colors; others stuck to just one color even though they examined the other bowls. Ultimately, the jellybeans didn't really "move" all that quickly.

When the researchers mixed up the beans and presented bowls of multicolor candy, the response was more enthusiastic — many more beans were taken when people didn't have to choose among so many different colors. The study group's "jellybean paralysis" went away when given what amounted to only one choice (no one picked individual colors out of the bowl). I can use this science. This is why I like putting dishes on a menu that have variety instead of forcing customers to choose among different variations on the theme. For example, I'll put chicken wings three ways (buffalo, Asian, and Jamaican jerk) on a single dish rather than list them as individual items. I sell about 25 percent more chicken wings when I do not force patrons to choose. Using my process, you can typically increase food revenue by 8 percent. When you increase the sales of your most profitable items, your food costs go down. Together, the combined dollar impact can be very significant. See the appendix for detailed tips on how to design great menus.

I can hear the peanut gallery saying, "Wait a minute . . . what about the phone-book-sized menus that characterize Greek diners and Jewish delis?" These old-fashioned American eateries are part of our cultural heritage; they fulfill the expectation of customers who are comforted by their abundance. But if you sit down and analyze their menus, you'll find that the copious amount of dishes offered are actually multiple variations on a fairly defined set of basic ingredients. And take another look at these food phone books, because they use the same boxing strategies I recommend. Bless their spanakopita and bagels with lox! Here's another thing: although I have not conducted a scientific study and I can find no statistics to back me up, in my thirty-five years of experience, I can tell you that most people go into a diner and order the same thing. The greater choice does not make them more experimental — it's the comfort in knowing their favorite deli can make three hundred versions of a corned beef sandwich that makes them feel good. But I'll take the pastrami on rye.

## Frequency Marketing

Part of the job of four-walls marketing is to entice people to come back — remember, you are shooting for the third and fourth visits. Once a customer walks through your door a fourth time, it means he has integrated your bar into his life. Repeat customers also have a propensity to tell other people about your place — regular customers provide free advertising that is powerful because it's authentic. Buying new customers through traditional advertising is expensive (about $40 to $70 a head), and the people who do respond to advertising have less than a 50 percent chance of returning for a second visit. So working with your existing customer base to build business is far less expensive and risky than trying to win new hearts and minds with a display ad in a newspaper or a thirty-second radio spot.

I wanted to increase repeat business at a restaurant in Arlington, Texas. To do it, I used the concept of "The Big Fat Claim." TBFC perks people up and makes them think, "Oh yeah? Prove it." At that point they're ready to listen to the rest of what I have to say; I've just gotten them to react the way I wanted them to react — with attention. We had a pretty amazing rib dish that was profitable too, so I wanted to sell more of it. I had postcards made up with a photograph of a barbecued rib on the front. On the back I made The Big Fat Claim that the restaurant had the best ribs in town, and to prove it, customers could try them for free. There were absolutely no restrictions on this offer.

I did a large mailing within the local area. I also motivated my staff to give the rib cards out by placing workers' initials on the backs of cards. Employees would take their initialed cards and distribute them around town. When the cards would come back, I'd check the initials and the server who got the most customers in would win $100. All a guest had to do was drop the card on the table when he came in, and he would get a free rib dinner. At that time the food cost was about $4.65 and the postcard cost $1 to design, print, and mail. Total price: $5.65—except that, unlike radio, newspapers, or other media advertising, the food didn't cost us any money until *the guest actually came in.* That card earned one visit from a customer, who was usually accompanied by one or more paying guests.

The staff had been trained to ask every customer whether it was her first time or a repeat visit. If the customer indicated it was her first time, the server would place a red beverage napkin on the table to flag the guest as new. Every staff member would now be aware of the first-time customers. If the customer had a free rib dinner card, so much the better. The card had captured a new customer. The manager was required to stop at every table that had a red napkin to ask how the customer had enjoyed her meal, including those who had ordered the free rib dinner.

"I'm glad you like them," he would say, and then add, "If you think the ribs are great, wait until you try the chicken." Then he would pull out a business card and write on the back "$5 off Chicken Dinner" to prompt her to return for a second visit. Note that this was not a preprinted discount card but rather a handwritten "discount" that made for a very personal reaction for the guest. It always makes a guest feel very special.

When the person arrived the second time — $5 discount card in hand — the server and the manager knew that this was a second-visit customer. When the check hit the table the manager (timing it perfectly) would come by again and ask the guest how she liked the chicken.

"It was great!" she'd say.

"I'll tell you what," the manager would reply. "Next time, save some room because you have to try our cheesecake. Let me write 'one piece of free cheesecake' on my card." He would initial the card and hand it to her. It all seemed very impromptu; however, it was completely contrived and planned to stimulate that third visit. The restaurant would earn a third visit from the customer and others like her. Once people come back for that third visit, the statistical likelihood of a fourth visit is *70 percent.*

That's one way you create frequency and regularity — and for a fraction of the cost per head of traditional advertising. I don't know why more businesses don't do it since it's very inexpensive. The rib dinner cost was $4.65, the postcard cost was $1, the chicken dinner cost was $5, and the cheesecake cost was $2. So from a statistical standpoint, I paid $12.65 to create a regular customer who, by the way, brought paying friends every time she walked through the door — so there's a chance her friends would become regulars too. For less than $13, I was able to get a customer to come back four times, which is a hell of a lot cheaper and so much more effective than prepaying between $40 and $70 per head to advertise for *one* visit. Yet so few people use this technique. From an economic standpoint, it is the cheapest way to market; from a marketing standpoint, it is the most effective way to market; and from a customer standpoint, it is beneficial — you build a relationship. People actually want to have relationships with the places where they eat and drink.

Bars can absolutely use TBFC to create frequency and traffic. A midlevel bar can offer "the best bar appetizer in the city, and to prove it, we will give you a free meatball appetizer." Or you can offer a free basket of the best hot wings around. Use the same red napkin technique to identify new customers. For a second visit, offer a two-for-one appetizer if they bring a friend. For the third visit, offer two bucks off a basket of wings. More upscale bar customers will not react as well to a card or a coupon, but they will react positively to a mailing that looks like a more formal and exclusive "invitation" — it's simply a matter of design and delivery. The offer and the premise are the same.

There are other ways bars can build on existing pools of customers. Here, some of my favorite proven winners:

### *Recurring Promotions Schedule*

I discourage one-night or one-day promotions in any business. The key to establishing frequency is to repeat the elements of your guest's experience that appealed to him in the first place. If a guest comes to your nightclub or bar on a Wednesday and experiences an appealing, motivating, and fun event, promotion, or product, he wants to come back and experience it again. If the following Wednesday (and other Wednesdays) has completely different products or entertainment — or none — your business will never develop guest loyalty for

Wednesday nights. This is true for any other night of the week, of course.

My approach involves developing promotional schedules that recur each mid-weeknight for at least eight consecutive weeks. All sorts of businesses use this technique: car washes have ladies' day, dry cleaners have men's suit day, the local family restaurant has Thursday as balloon day for kids. The science behind the strategy comes from the way we create habits. If you can get people to remember that Monday is half-price microbrew beer day at your bar, you will get a great crowd on Monday nights — and many of them are not going to even order the half-price beer.

Recurring promotions provides a basis to grow your business each week, over several weeks, as you develop relationships with guests who come for that promotion or night. To be profitable, you need to grow your guest traffic by a couple of percentage points each week (typically between six and fifteen people more each week) to realize terrific results over two or three months. A recurring promotional format gives you the basis to do so.

### *Festivals and Week- and Monthlong Events*

There are so many opportunities for bars to exploit what is called in the industry a "limited time offer," or LTO, which are often marketed as monthlong events. Choose themes that fit the members of your audience whom you want to attract. Bars can hold so many different kinds of events and they don't have to involve lower prices. For instance, you can work with your wine distributor to orchestrate a wine festival that features seasonal wines, wines from certain wineries, or special kinds of wine, like burgundies or pinot noirs, and so on. Tastings can feature several two-ounce glasses of wine—it's actually a great way for guests to taste a lot of high-end wines that they may not get a chance to try often or at all.

Football week at a sports bar can feature games and other football-oriented shows when no live games are on. Just remember that you need to show sports in a sports bars—two guys talking about last night's game behind a desk doesn't cut it. Invest in a sports package that enables you to provide continuous action-packed games or sporting events, whatever they are. Appropriate food and beverage promotions can be offered with a beer distributor. A fashion week will attract women customers, and for this kind of event you might offer "skinny" cocktail tastings and special "small plates" menu items. In the summer, outside deck festivals featuring live music can be a draw. Likewise, "winter blues" festivals can bring people in even when it's freezing outside—if you offer an interesting selection of warm cocktails.

Never underestimate the enthusiasm of distributors and suppliers to help you create great events that help to promote or sell their brands. Distributors often have ideas for events and supporting marketing material (posters, flyers, giveaways) that make it easy to arrange these special celebrations. A Smirnoff Vodka Festival, Captain Morgan's Rum Fest, or Guinness Beer Garden Week, or promoting Bushmills Whiskey Wednesdays for a month, can bring in different crowds during different time periods. These events should not conflict with your weekly promotional schedule. Rather, they should complement them by adding something even more appealing to your guest experience.

When planning, consider that the word "festival" may not be the best word for your event. Be creative and come up with a name for your event that gets noticed. How about "gala," "fiesta," "carnival," "fair," "celebration," "party," "Mardi Gras"? You get the picture—there are many ways to express a limited time event. Remember, if you're not noticed, you're invisible!

### *Bounce Back Incentive Programs*

Bounce backs or incentive promotions can take any delivery approach. They could be embossed invitations for chef or wine tastings in an upscale bar, or a voucher for a free sandwich or a basket of cheese fries in a more casual place. At the end of the day, guess what? They're *both* coupons that have been designed for two different audiences and markets. With effective creativity, there is no reason why a bounce back incentive program cannot be used for any concept or audience in any situation. Nightclubs can take many approaches, including "private" invitations to "preopening premieres" (earlier evening)—wine, buffet, or martini tastings, or other special, often complimentary events—before nightly promotions. Other nightclub opportunities include door passes, VIP admission, beverage tickets, free "reserved table" confirmations, or complimentary bottle service for groups (e.g., bring in five friends and the bar will give you one bottle to get the group started). These can be very effective.

### *Periodic Themes and Menus*

Nightclubs should consider making environmental changes a few times a year to exploit the seasons. Changing some visual elements can keep interest and keep your environment fresh. For example, summer outfits (tropical shirts, bikinis, etc.), winter looks, and other seasonal costumes can be very effective. Always introduce new products to support these changes and to maximize your sales results. Again, consider seasonal events such as the PGA or the US Open, the start of football or baseball season, Fashion Week, the Emmys or Oscars, and so on.

### *Step Outside the Box*

Like many, I've made a lot of money with NFL-based promotions over the years. When we sought out and formed our own in-house fan clubs for teams outside our markets (Packer Backers, True Blue Cowboy clubs, etc.), we really grew the Sunday afternoon bar business. But it was a very different story for *Monday Night Football* promotions. Guys tend to stay home to watch the game on television on Monday nights, so our promotions on those evenings were not highly effective. I took a different approach and launched "I Hate Football Mondays" and "Chicks Against Football Mondays." We still had the game on the monitors, but we targeted all our promotional ideas and outreach to females. We were the only operation on Mondays to be filled with women. Ever see a bar or nightclub with a couple of hundred females go broke? Me neither.

## Staff Appearance

Server clothing is the last decision you make once the menu is done, because the food and drink determine what kind of physical demands will be placed on staff members — I'm not going to put white shirts on people who will be serving pasta dishes with red sauce, for instance. Staff appearance is part of four-walls marketing, so whatever you choose should make sense and relate to your bar's concept. I'm not talking about putting your staff in ridiculous outfits — in fact, most of the time I do very simple T-shirts or button-down shirts. At Downey's, I did logo ties; at Racks, I did low-cut red T-shirts. A server at Morton's would never wear jeans, just as a bartender at a sports bar would never wear wool dress pants.

An actor puts on a costume and performs — this was the attitude Walt Disney took toward his park employees. He saw them as cast members, entertainers who played roles for the public. I'm with Walt; I like "costume" so much better than the word "uniform" and its rigid implications. When servers or bartenders think of themselves as wearing a costume, they have a different perspective on the job they are doing — it actually does increase the effectiveness of all the dynamics they've learned.

I want to talk about Hooters again here because, even though it's a punch line to a lot of jokes, the company has a very interesting approach to costume. Believe me, as a former owner of two Hooters, I can tell you appearance standards play a vital part in the chain's four-walls marketing. The Hooters appearance standards are very detailed and precise. Waitresses wear the same shorts and T-shirt; they wear the exact same Skechers sneakers, the same socks, the same standard bra style, and the same Hooters-approved pantyhose, sold from a vending machine in the back of every restaurant. Nail polish, earrings, hairstyles, makeup — the standards for every aspect of a waitress's appearance is defined and explained so nothing is left to chance. In fact, the dressing room in the back of the restaurant has posters illustrating how nails should look, how to cover tattoos, and so on.

The real benefit of the Hooters costume is that customers can tell with a glance which women are waitresses. When you can't tell the servers from the customers, it's a problem. I ran a business where the servers wore name tags but otherwise wore a simple outfit that came from their own wardrobes. If they did not have a name tag, they could not go out on the floor, because it was the only distinguishing feature that let customers know the person was a member of the staff. I kept ten name tags with different names on a bulletin board in my office. If someone forgot his tag, he would pay a two-dollar "rental fee" to use one of mine. That went into a big jar in my office, and when it filled up we'd use the proceeds for staff parties. It was a good way of reminding people of their responsibility to the "costume," which in this case was pretty simple.

During the second season of *Bar Rescue,* I helped a very sad bikini bar in California called Extremes Sports Bar and Grill. The only thing extreme about it was the owner's drinking and how it affected the way he managed the place. There is absolutely nothing wrong with bikini bars, and in the right market they can be moneymakers. There's also nothing wrong with sexy cocktail waitresses—the problem was that the girls at Extremes wore their own bikini outfits and there was no consistency or level of taste. Some of them wore bra tops with short shorts that were very revealing; others wore bikini bathing suits. The women did not look professional and they certainly didn't feel very comfortable.

We transformed Extremes into a sexy sports bar named Second Base. It was one mile from Angels Stadium in Anaheim, so we pinstriped the building like a baseball uniform. We had to do something about the way the women servers looked, of course. I had special costumes made that consisted of short, tight-bottomed shorts that gave full coverage and were pinstriped like the building. A coordinating bathing suit bikini top that was sexy but also provided full coverage completed the outfit. All the women loved it because they felt attractive as well as decent. I call this approachable sexuality. When a server had to bend over she felt comfortable, not exposed — the clothing changed the attitudes of the servers and the patrons.

## Presentation and Plating

How you serve your food and beverages is a device that reinforces the story of your bar. I'm not a five-star chef, so this isn't a lesson in creating towering salads and elaborate plate paintings with velvety sauces. Rather, I want you to think about the visual presentation of food and what message you're conveying when it is placed in front of a guest. Plates do not have to be feats of architectural achievement in order to make a person stop talking to his companion and appreciate and be enticed by the food in front of him. I have sent back plates to be replated numerous times until they achieve the stop-what-you're-doing reaction I want. Even the simplest food program can benefit from a little effort in managing the cook and getting him to improve plating specifications. The appealing encounter — that moment of delight when the food arrives — that your guests have with your food, starting with its presentation, is another marketing tool to create loyalty and repeat business.

Don't worry — creative plating is not difficult to achieve and doesn't take special training. All you have to do is exceed the envelope of expectation people have about how food should look when it comes out of the kitchen. Neatness counts — all good cooks wipe edges clean of dressing or sauce, and food should be mounded or piled in such a way that it doesn't look as if it were tossed on the plate from a long distance. That should be the easiest and most basic part of standards you've set for your kitchen staff.

There are a few elements you should focus on: height always sells, color creates excitement, and playfulness promotes an emotion connection. If you can achieve those three things on a plate, you're halfway there. The food, of course, has to taste good! When a plate passes by you in a restaurant, you will notice it if it has any height at all, while a plate that has a low profile remains that way. It will not catch your eye. Height gives a plate movement and excitement. When defining plating for each dish on your menu, think about the elements that can be raised. Fries can be piled in such a way as to form a pyramid; a green salad can likewise be piled high, starting with a wide base of lettuce that works its way up to a peak. One of my favorite ways to create height in a casual dining environment is to stack onion rings on a standing stick. In one situation, I used a small baseball bat and stacked the rings on it — which provided both height and a sense of play.

A three-color plate is standard. Any more than that and the plate starts to get busy. Get creative when devising edible items you can add to the top of French fries, mashed potatoes, or other food. Fresh chopped parsley or cilantro and grated lemon rind make for a tasty garnish; julienned red and orange peppers look great piled atop an open-faced burger; carrot and zucchini ribbons are whimsical and provide a burst of fresh color atop a simple pasta dish. You get the idea — just remember the rule of three.

Playfulness has endless opportunities. I like using the knuckle side of chicken wings and putting them on the menu as "little sluggers" because they mimic miniature baseball bats. "Branding" the top of a sandwich or burger bun with the initials of your business is memorable and cute. Small branding irons are very easy to find online. In a casual venue that specializes in barbecue, burgers, or comfort food, serving entrées on a tin-pie plate adds to the story and experience you're creating. I like to serve shrimp cocktails in oversized martini glasses, with the tails hooked around the edges and the small vessels of sauce in the middle. For family-oriented or beach bars, I use Frisbees with the bar's logo, address, and phone number printed on the top. Flip them over, line them with wax or parchment paper, and they're great plates for casual food — and guests can take them home.

Not every type of beverage service needs to adhere to strict glassware rules. You really need only six or seven basic glasses to accommodate red and white wine, beer, ale, short and long cocktails, and straight cocktails. Why not make those glasses unique? If you order a martini straight up, it should come in a stemmed glass — this is within our envelope of expectation. Why not use an unusual version of that glass, perhaps one with a colored stem or no stem at all, or a monogram on the front?

If you serve draft beer, you have to use the right vessel, but acceptable mug or pint glasses come in creative variations. When we worked on the Chicken Bone, we visited the Samuel Adams Brewery and its founder, Jim Koch, who supplied the bar with beer glasses that were laser cut on the bottom. This design actually helps aerate the beer, so when you take a sip the bubbles subtly hit your nose along with a nice aroma. Not only does the glass improve the customer's enjoyment, but it also gives the bartender a great story to tell — a way to engage the customer. When I do a couples-oriented bar or restaurant, we encourage togetherness by making cocktails in a small fishbowl with two straws. It's served in the middle of the table so the couple can sip from it at the same time. It's fun and purposeful. In fact, all glassware, like plating, should serve marketing and merchandising objectives.

As for plates and other serving vessels, I understand that many chefs recommend white, but I am not a stickler. Color is fine as long as it enhances the food and does not detract from it. The food is what you're selling, not the plate. I like hip, modern plates. Look for unusual shapes (square, triangular, oblong), perhaps with some embossing or pattern. Avoid printed or garish plates, because the food disappears. Likewise, colored glasses don't let the customer see the beverage—and the visual aspect is a huge part of enjoying a great cocktail. In short, have some fun and experiment. Find tableware that contributes to the strengths of both your menu and your market. You can't go wrong unless you're a bore.

In summary, customer frequency and sales growth are driven by three key elements of four-walls marketing:

**Guest Experience.** I can't emphasize this enough. All four-walls marketing efforts must establish positive customer reactions and help turn transactions into positive reactions.

**Great Customer Service.** Attention to detail is key—set the bar as high as you can and reach it every time. It's all about reactions.

**Consistency.** The level of follow-through and standards that consistency requires is an investment worth making. You do not measure your success; the reactions of your guests do.

# 6

# Interior Works

The essence of interior design will always be about people and how they live. It is about the realities of what makes for an attractive, civilized, meaningful environment, not about fashion or what's in or what's out. This is not an easy job.

— ALBERT HADLEY, INTERIOR DESIGNER

RETIRED BANKER TIM EYERLY bought the Orange, California, working-class bar the Olive Pit in 2001. In the first couple of years under Eyerly's ownership, the bar turned a profit and brought in about $50,000 a month thanks mainly to a loyal core of regulars and local groups of college kids. When Tim began neglecting the property and behaving improperly (inappropriate behavior with waitresses, drinking on the job), even the faithful became disillusioned. Bars can't thrive on the patronage of regulars alone, but if that's all you've got and they start to migrate, you've got problems. A bar has to attract a constant flow of new customers. Every bar and business has attrition, and in California the attrition rate is higher than in other places. You have to generate 20 percent new business every month to mitigate attrition, and sometimes more, just to stay even. If you do not, you will find guest counts go down. A perfect business is about 20 percent new customers and 80 percent repeat customers.

When I heard about the Olive Pit, it was about to celebrate its fiftieth anniversary — this was an opportune moment to fix its troubles and get it back in the black. Taffer team bar and hospitality specialist Kat Munday and chef Brian Duffy helped identify the many issues Eyerly's unprofessionalism had created. Our first impressions confirmed what Nicole had already described ("I expected a rat to run through the room") after her initial recon visit. "Ugly" was an insufficient descriptor. The public areas of the bar were clad in repulsive fake paneling punctuated by strange-looking pockmarks. The floor was so encrusted with dirt, I wasn't even sure what it was made of. Moving on, there were several fist-sized holes in the walls; peeling stickers with beer logos slapped onto every conceivable surface to hide more holes; harsh, flickering fluorescent lighting; and dingy, barely functioning washrooms. Capping off the experience was the stench of mildew mixed with stale alcohol.

Behind the open bar, we discovered clogged beer tap lines, putrefied mats stuck to the back bar, a corroded bar top, and shards of broken glass in the well — disastrous conditions in full view of customers. In the kitchen, Chef Duffy found a walk-in cooler laced with black mold, an inoperable range hood caked with grease, and an expired 2010 fire certification ticket tacked to the wall. If owner Eyerly and his daughter, Tracy, hadn't invited me to rescue the Olive Pit, I would have considered the suggestion to set a match to it a pretty good idea.

Honestly, it was astounding that this dump was still open, since it was breaking nearly every health code and a few employment laws. I'm not sure how the Olive Pit managed to avoid the scrutiny of city health inspectors for so long. I've seen some pretty gross interiors in my time, and I describe quite a few here, but this one was over the top. I am not overstating it when I tell you that I felt unsafe just standing in this place without wearing a hazmat suit. It was that disgusting.

Let me be clear — the interior of a bar does not have to be conventionally handsome or trendy to suit its intended purpose. But even the divey-est of dive bars have to be well kept and clean and observe basic health codes. Beyond that, the mission of a bar's interior design is simple: to encourage repeat business and increase guest length of stay. That's it. The longer guests stay, the more they spend. Bar design plays an important role in achieving this goal. Form must truly follow function and comfort. Unfortunately, I see too many bar designs that allow function to follow form or, in the case of the Olive Pit, formlessness.

Putting aside the filth for a minute, from a purely functional point of view, Eyerly's bar was a failure. The dark, dank interior held little appeal for women and in fact scared most of them off. The bar and nightclub industry could not survive without women. The cavernous, disjointed, and cluttered space suffered from uncomfortable seating and a confused floor plan. A long drink rail lined the perimeter of the room, providing plenty of places to sit — except all the chairs faced the wall. How does that promote social interaction and reactions necessary to increase length of stay and sales? The bar had a sharp corner, which caused servers to face away from most guests when preparing or pouring a beverage.

The configuration of the bar blocked the sight line of people sitting opposite each other, which made flirting (I know, a long shot in this place) impossible. The setup discouraged length of stay and it certainly didn't inspire reorders or repeat business. I've never once in my career heard a guest say, "Let's spend an evening at that repulsive bar where it's impossible to make eye contact." Various game tables blocked movement because they were placed in the middle of the room, compounding the sense of confusion. There was no distinction between bar and recreation areas. Uncertainty diminishes sales.

In the course of filming the episode, we transformed the newly minted O.P. into a clean, hip, and updated dive bar that is now both comfortable and cheerful. Dark wood flooring and new wallpaper reminiscent of 1960s pop art design give the place a mod, fun feel. Retro fixtures with flattering incandescent warmth make women customers look better. Better lighting also creates a spacious and inviting atmosphere in what is essentially a windowless basement. The pinball machines, video terminals, and pool tables were moved into a designated game area away from the bar, which promotes flow and clearly indicates the various social areas the bar offers.

Now the O.P. décor encourages people to stick around, have fun, and spend money. That is the mission of customer-centric interior design.

> Bars offer a distinctive social experience. Sure, you can make drinks more cheaply at home, watch cable TV, or stare at Facebook. The one thing you can't get at home is an authentic personal social interaction. No matter how far society "progresses," our thirst for community and connection will never diminish. Bars satisfy this need.

## Define Your Direction

Some years ago, Peter Quarelli, the owner of a western-themed bar called Pistol Pete's Steakhouse and Saloon in Pleasantville, New Jersey, called me for advice.

"Jon," he said, "I'm losing a fortune, but I have the only mechanical bull in New Jersey. I should be getting rich!"

"Pete," I said, "you're not making money *because* you have the only mechanical bull in New Jersey." A mechanical bull in Pleasantville, New Jersey, is certainly an unexpected attraction, but it isn't the right one. It was a turnoff. We pulled out the bull and made other adjustments to the interior and Pistol Pete's succeeded for many years. (Sadly, I discovered recently that Pete filed for Chapter 11 bankruptcy protection, later changing the status to Chapter 7 liquidation, an outcome that news reports linked to the restaurant's liability in a motorcycle accident.)

Don't get me wrong—I'm all for theme bars, and I believe they can work if designed and marketed appropriately. Mega brands like Hard Rock Cafe and Planet Hollywood benefit from tremendous consumer recognition. A tiki bar right on the beach, sure, that makes sense. Ethnic themes (Mexican, Indian, Asian) are universally appreciated and can work well almost anywhere, especially those that avoid the pitfall of using outdated and unsophisticated interpretations of foreign aesthetics and cuisine. Even a western bar can find an audience in New Jersey, if it's done in a way that the community can relate to.

It's when themes become highly specific that marketing and sales challenges become harder to surmount. I once went to a bar that had covered its walls with the previously worn shoes of famous people. Do you want to have a drink and a bite to eat next to a pair of worn-out shoes? I didn't think so. Needless to say, the bar failed. How about a fun idea, like a pirate bar? That kind of place could work very well in St. Petersburg, Florida, or even in San Francisco. But how about in Maryland? Call me skeptical, but I don't believe that's a sustainable combination. When I accepted an invitation to rescue the $900,000-in-debt Piratz Tavern in downtown Silver Spring, there were many problems, but the interior design, driven by its pirate theme, was one of the bigger obstacles. There is no pirate tradition in Silver Spring, just as there is no bull wrangling in Pleasantville, New Jersey.

More than that, the bar's articulation of "pirate" was a complete failure — random, cluttered, nonsensical, dirty, low quality. A stranger happening upon Piratz would be utterly confused and somewhat disturbed by the violent nature of many of the doodads, novelty items, and figurines covering every surface. I don't think even a real pirate would want any booty from this place. There is actually a way to "do" pirate that is fun and tasteful, but Piratz had obviously missed that day at pirate school. Check out Smuggler's Cove in San Francisco if you doubt me — *Travel + Leisure* named it one of America's best cocktail bars. A temple to rum. The small tropical oasis has a fifty-person capacity on three floors and features more than 170 rums, which are used in imaginative Prohibition-era Havana classics and California tiki cocktails from the 1950s. Smuggler's Cove is beautiful, tasteful, well run, and very successful.

At any rate, Piratz was on the verge of shutting down not because hoards of people walked through the door but didn't return (which would have indicated a solvable systemic problem, not a theme issue), but because very few *non-pirates* (i.e., normal people) walked through the door in the first place. And the place needed regular people to survive. Of course, the non-pirates who stumbled into the bar also didn't return (demonstrating both a systemic and a pirate problem). There weren't enough pretend pirates in the whole region to take up the slack. You see, during a staff meeting, owner Tracy Rebelo revealed to me that the bar did actually target Silver Spring's "pirate community." I said, "Great, where do you find them?" She told me they had a Facebook page with two hundred fans. If you haven't realized this by now, you cannot run a successful bar based on a target audience of two hundred people.

I changed the bar to a theme that I believed would appeal to the daytime office workers who descended on the area Monday through Friday. Piratz was in an ideal location to serve these people lunch and happy hour. At night, the neighborhood was desolate. We renamed the bar Corporate and created a sleek, modern interior that communicated professional, efficient service — pace is important with a working crowd because office workers have to be back at their desks in a timely fashion.

Problem was, Tracy wasn't happy — I learned only after the fact that she'd had a bad personal experience with corporate life, so my theme, which I still stand behind 100 percent, was particularly difficult for her to accept on an emotional level. After the *Bar Rescue* crew left, Tracy staged a public burning of the new sign we had made for the bar and reverted the venue back to its original concept. My prediction is that Piratz will fail. The only way a theme and design can work is if it suits your dominant audience.

This is a cautionary tale for those of you who are tempted to focus on a highly distinctive décor inspired by a personal fetish or fanatical hobby. Reconsider. Why would you want to force your business into a very small design box that will appeal to only a very limited group of people, too easily falls prey to cliché, gets dated very quickly, is expensive to renew, and narrowly defines your objective? Why not give yourself some conceptual breathing room with a more loosely defined idea that's easier to both execute and understand? I believe the bad execution and faulty market analysis were Piratz Tavern's fatal flaws.

You can fix the food, elevate mixology standards, improve service quality, and clean what's dirty at a troubled bar. But the challenges built into highly personal themes with no built-in audience imprison owners, and that's a tragedy. At the Blue Frog 22, or the Local, as we renamed it, the theme was vintage children's toys and games. But it was an adult bar in an adult neighborhood. Grown-ups just could not relate to the trucks and dolls and teddy bears that hung from the ceiling and sat on every available shelf. The theme was perhaps not coincidentally symbolic of an underlying family issue at the bar—co-owners Mimi Witschy and John Reed were mother and son. Mimi had a very hard time allowing John to take over management of the business even though it—and she—was failing badly. Getting rid of the toy theme was not like taking candy from a baby, however. It took some convincing to lose the kid stuff and convince Mimi to hand the reins to her son.

Go ahead and latch on to a concept! Just be smart about it: embrace your community's local history, let your general interests (cars, travel, fishing . . .) inspire your bar, but don't let them get a stranglehold on it. A bar business is not the place to work through your psychodrama. When you hit on an idea you think could work, play around with various ways you could express it. As you build out your concept, remember that an interior should deliver familiarity without dullness, depth without complexity, and it should offer an experience with perceived value. Keep it simple. A great bar interior has at least three different finishes or textures.

Romano's Macaroni Grill creates an authentic and relatable Italian feeling with stone details and other natural materials, and warm, muted tones, but doesn't get tripped up by kitsch that other Italian chains fall victim to. The multiple textures at the Macaroni Grill are elevating in nature — and that helps the acceptance level of elevated prices. Celebrity chef Mario Batali's bar-restaurants are great examples of simplicity: the interior designs of Babbo, Casa Mono, and Esca transport diners to Rome, Barcelona, and Sicily, respectively, using a deceptively effortless classicism and attention to detail.

Simplicity has other advantages. It's easy to tweak when your bar needs an update, and customers are less prone to boredom. T.G.I. Friday's is a good example of this. When the bar-restaurant first opened, it was known for quirky, vintage, multilayered décor. It has streamlined and simplified the interior look since that time — but Friday's is still Friday's. Simple is also profitable. It's a quality that motivates customers to move from "just looking" to buy, according to a study published in the *Harvard Business Review*. Researchers and authors Patrick Spenner and Karen Freeman found that brands that scored the highest in terms of simplicity were 86 percent more likely to be purchased by consumers than those that scored the lowest. Simpler products were 9 percent more likely to be repurchased and 115 percent more apt to be recommended to others. That's powerful information for hopeful bar entrepreneurs to keep in mind.

Bars create a sensory experience rather than an intellectual one. To manage this experience, consider how customers perceive what they see and hear rather than what they know or might believe—information you don't have ready access to anyway. That means you are managing customers' perceptions by manipulating what they see, touch and feel, hear, smell, and taste.

## Full Throttle

Earlier I said the purpose of a bar's interior is to support and maximize length of stay. The longer a guest enjoys her outing, the bigger her tab. Bars are somewhat unique in this regard, compared to restaurants, where turnover generally trumps time spent. Restaurants seat customers at least two times per table during meal shifts. Management has to make sure tables are served and cleared within a reasonable amount of time to make way for another party. Restaurants walk a fine line because a successful eatery can't make a guest feel rushed. Turnover and courtesy is a delicate balance.

Ultra-expensive fine dining experiences like the Four Seasons in New York City can afford to let guests draw out a meal—up to two hours and forty-five minutes—because its average two-person tab is around $500. Compare that to the national average cost of dinner for two, about $72, and the average length of stay, about ninety minutes. Less costly establishments have to make each table work a little harder, not just through up-selling the menu but also through additional seating. Lingering doesn't pay because, in general, restaurant customers don't order more once the plates have been cleared and coffee has been served. A restaurant's "throttles"—table configuration; when the menu is offered, the order is taken, the food is served, the place setting cleared, and so on—are designed to maximize ordering per table *and* parties served per table per shift.

Bar throttles, or customer service standards, engage customers in a very different way. While the polite interruptions of a waiter are carefully timed to progress a meal to its natural conclusion (your departure), the solicitous tugs of a good bartender are intended to *suspend* time, so that you stay another thirty minutes and order another glass of wine. A bar doesn't predetermine a conclusion to a guest encounter; departure is deliberately open-ended, dictated only by last call. The environment (lighting, seating heights, and music volume and tempo) should support this goal. When two colleagues go to a bar to catch up or blow off steam, the comfort of the environmental components largely determine how deep and long that conversation will be. Likewise, the couple looking for an evening of romance spends more time feeding each other finger food and sipping cocktails if the setting enhances their personal intimacy. The dance club designed to increase flow, positive energy, and fast, friendly service keeps friends partying (and ordering) into the night.

The whole point of interior bar design is to move the customers' eyes around the room, creating anticipation and positive reactions. There are also five physical or sensory dynamics that are critical to creating positive emotional guest reactions and maximizing their length of stay. These throttles address where a guest's eyes go and what her reaction is to what she sees (the pace of the staff, tabletops and back bar appearance), what she hears and how she reacts and connects to it (oldies, hip hop, jazz), and what she smells and how it makes her feel. Pure emotion.

According to Harvard Business School professor and consumer behavior expert Gerald Zaltman, *95 percent* of a purchasing decision is based on an emotional response rather than rational deliberation. That is great news for bars because you can control these five throttles for optimal emotional guest reactions. People might go online to compare the price of flat-screen TVs before buying one, but they don't analyze who has the cheapest beer before going out. Price is not why a person chooses to spend time in one bar over another—that decision is probably 100 percent emotional. If your five throttles meet your customers' needs, you will realize a sales increase of 8 percent or more. The five throttles are: upkeep, guest comfort and flow, bar dynamics, lighting, and music/entertainment and sound quality.

### *Upkeep*

In the first twenty seconds after a customer steps into a bar, he gets all the information he needs to make a lasting judgment of your business—and it all has to do with that initial impression of how clean your place looks and smells. It sounds like an absolute no-brainer to list sanitation as a factor in the success of a bar's interior "design," but it is not. Lax cleaning standards are common to failing bars—this is obvious if you watch *Bar Rescue*—and clearly demonstrate the devastating consequences neglect has on a business. Sadly, maintenance is often one of the first controls to spin out when a bar starts to run into trouble. There is no clearer sign of a business in decline than the condition of its fittings and furnishings.

Atmosphere, cleanliness, and friendly service top of the list of most important attributes, according to Technomic, an independent consumer research firm. The company asked eighteen thousand active restaurant consumers to rank fifty hospitality attributes in importance. Surprisingly, the diners ranked cleanliness of glassware, dishware, and silverware as being *number one* in importance—93 percent identified it as their top concern. In the list of top ten attributes, "cleanliness" made an appearance three more times, with consumers placing a high value on an overall clean interior, bathrooms, and visible prep areas. This concern goes directly to repeat business and length of stay.

Establishments with the highest cleanliness scores had "higher intent to return" scores. Chains that landed in the top 25 percent of tableware cleanliness satisfaction saw same-location sales growth of 4 percent. Those with very low tableware cleanliness satisfaction scores averaged only 0.2 percent sales growth during the same time period. As an example of how dirty tableware can kill frequency, if a business serves two hundred customers a day, sixty-seven would not return to the establishment if they felt it was unsanitary, according to the research. A majority of them would share their displeasure with friends and family, who would also be discouraged from visiting your bar. According to surveys commissioned by SCA, a large manufacturer of sixty international, regional, and local personal care products, 74 percent of adults equate restroom cleanliness with the cleanliness of a restaurant's kitchen. Nearly a third of American adults would not return to a location with a dirty washroom.

Liquor bottles, ice, and cut-up fruit kept in the visible bar area have to be pristine. There's no greater thirst killer than the sight of fruit flies swarming around open bottles and trays filled with brown, wilted produce. At Rocks in Laguna Niguel, California, I discovered that the bartenders would put plastic wrap around the pour stems on all the open liquor bottles because they were more interested in their own convenience than the customers' experience. Think about it—how would you react if you saw that all the bottles behind a bar were wearing little plastic hats?

When a bar has a fruit fly problem, plastic wrap is a common solution to keep the flies from contaminating the spouts and laying eggs. This can be a helpful practice overnight, but most people have enough brains to remove the wrapping when the bar is open. It's a much better idea not to give insects a reason to invade your place: make sure spouts have built-in removable caps and keep pour spouts, along with the rest of the bar area, spotless.

The ice machine holds great potential for bacterial infestation. Many bar staffers think that the cold temperature kills bacteria. Wrong. Bacteria are actually preserved in ice until conditions "improve" as the ice melts and activates these living organisms. Viruses, I should note, are basically impervious to cold. Bare hands should never be used to put ice in a glass. Nor should a glass be used as a scoop because it is a good vehicle for germs to get into the bin if the server forgot to wash his hands. (And, as I noted previously, the glass can also break in the bin and then get scooped into a drink.) A long-handled scoop should be used to serve ice, and the handle should never touch the ice or edges of the bin.

A laundry service can take care of cotton and linen tablecloths, napkins, and any other products — but it's expensive, from 50¢ to $1.50 per piece. So think carefully about your budget before investing in linens. Does your bar's concept demand cloth napkins? There are numerous cleaning and maintenance contractors and companies that specifically service the hospitality industry. Find and hire one if you or your staff can't keep up with maintenance.

If your bar is carpeted, have the carpets shampooed on a regular basis. Wood floors should be sealed and maintained with proper cleaning fluids, and refreshed or refinished when necessary. Wood is porous, so if it isn't sealed properly, it will absorb bacteria, mold, and odors. Stone, tile, concrete, or synthetic flooring should also be washed every day and maintained and repaired frequently. For those establishments with high ceilings, exposed beams should be cleaned and dusted regularly to remove buildup, spiderwebs, and so on. Water-damaged or broken tiles on the ceiling have to be repaired or replaced as soon as possible. Keep a ladder handy for this task, and while you're up there, wipe lighting fixtures and ceiling fans.

Teach best cleaning practices and make them part of your staff's daily routine. Embed cleanliness in your culture. This is a nonnegotiable. Otherwise it's far too easy for people to get lazy and blow off maintenance tasks. Hold everyone accountable, including yourself, for best sanitation practices. Encourage, no *demand,* staff members to speak up if and when they see a bad practice. *You* have to take responsibility and regularly spot-check silverware, glassware, dishware, floors, furniture, tables and other surfaces, and restrooms at multiple points during shifts. Make repairs to upholstery and other furniture, fixtures, walls, windows, and so on as soon as possible — a hole in an upholstered barstool may seem minor, but it sends a negative message to guests.

### *Personal Responsibility*

When you own or run a bar, you have a serious responsibility to provide a safe space. The public places its trust in establishments and that trust should be honored. Don't risk your customers' health or your livelihood by operating anything less than a clean establishment. I regularly shut restaurants down when I see kitchen employees who don't follow standard procedures to eliminate cross-contamination after handling raw meats or using the restroom. This puts everyone in a bar at risk of serious illness and, potentially, death. This is no joke.

When my daughter, Samantha, went into J.A. Murphy's Tavern

to do recon for me, the hidden camera in the kitchen showed the cook handling raw chicken with her bare hands and then putting her hands into a container of shredded cheese without bothering to wash up in between. My daughter was seconds away from eating this food. I was furious and stormed out of the control room to stop her from putting it in her mouth. That cook got an earful from me. Food-borne illnesses that can be transferred through employees' hands alone include *E. coli*, norovirus, and hepatitis A. During an inspection of Murphy's, I saw cutting boards that were not separated by use and furthermore were being used interchangeably to cut meat and produce. Mouse droppings were everywhere — in food containers, on the floor, and inside appliances.

Contaminated food and drink usually tastes and smells bad — and believe me, those things do not increase length of stay. They generally increase speed of departure. Check, please! That's the least of it. A food-borne illness event can ruin your reputation. The National Restaurant Association estimates that a single outbreak of a food-related illness can cost an establishment about $75,000. Lawsuit costs against establishments that have gotten people sick have ranged from $150,000 to nearly $5 million. Even the *suggestion* that a bar has sanitation issues can put it out of business. I believe the reputation for filth was one of the irreversible problems at the renamed Murphy's Law, making it hard for the co-owners to stay in business even after we had cleaned up the bar and kitchen and given them the proper tools and information to maintain high standards in the front and back of the house.

Glasses must be washed at a minimum temperature of 171 degrees Fahrenheit or with chemical sanitizers in a low-temperature dishwasher. Low-temp dishwashers don't always remove lipstick from glasses, so your dish machine operator has to be vigilant in checking for and removing stains when glassware come out of a wash cycle. Serving a drink with a stranger's Revlon #457 on the rim is unacceptable. Store glassware properly on racks or fishnet plastic sheeting so that it stays dust and grease free. Beer taps and plastic beer tubes also have to be maintained for hygiene. Draft systems are susceptible to contaminants like yeast, mold, and bacteria. These contaminants degrade the taste and aroma of beer, which can decrease guest length of stay — how long is a customer going to hang out if your beer stinks or tastes off? Draft beer systems should be cleaned out twice a month as part of a regular maintenance schedule.

### *Guest Comfort and Flow*

When a guest feels "at home" and relaxed, she wants to settle in and stay awhile. Promoting this feeling has everything to do with offering comfortable seating and a floor plan that provides breathing and elbow room as well as ease of movement, while also encouraging mingling and eye contact. The "softer" the amenities of an interior, the longer a customer stays. Softer finishes not only slow the pace, they justify charging higher prices. Barstools and chairs should be ample enough to accommodate a range of shapes and sizes — diminutive chairs make even average-sized men and women feel awkward and unattractive. Banquettes should be high-backed and firm enough to support someone's back in comfort, but not so hard that she can't find a comfortable sitting position. Seating has to be interactive. If it's too low ("Hugh Hefner seating," as we call it), it can work against you, because the customer is so low he feels intimidated . . . and who wants to sit on a couch only to find himself staring at a bunch of asses?

Consider your *primary* customer when selecting barstools. She is the one who you want to cater to first. If the female demographic of a bar is over thirty-four years old, I use barstools with backs. If the female demographic is under thirty-four years old, I don't. Why? Because as women get older, they become more sensitive about their backs, while younger women want to be more interactive. They want to be able to swing around and talk to people behind them and on either side of them. We actually replaced the barstools at Swanky Bubbles/Sheer because their backs blocked social interaction. Keep in mind that chairs with backs take up more room than those without. Since Sheer was directed at younger people, sleeker backless stools that encouraged interaction were more appropriate — and they also increased seating capacity at the bar without overcrowding it.

When customers avoid entire areas of a bar, valuable real estate is wasted. The two major reasons why customers don't naturally flow into certain areas of a space is because they can't see and define them immediately, or they look like dead ends. Floor plans and furniture layout must allow people to survey the bar when they first come in the room and to "see a way out" by creating a visible loop around the end of a room. Say you have steps up to another seating area — if people can only see the stairs and then a back wall with no obvious way to get out of the area, they will absolutely not want to use that space.

People must have open sight lines in bars and nightclubs. This is why when an architect shows me a blueprint with a lot of lines on it, I ask a lot of questions. Lines mean walls, and not only do I not want to waste $100 per linear foot on an unnecessary wall, but I also do not want to lose valuable customer interaction because a wall gets in the way of a good time. Walls that cut rooms in half or interrupt sight lines typically decrease guest enjoyment and comfort. Vantage points or viewing windows to televisions that are divided or obscured by half walls create conflict among customers, which leads to frustration and decreased stay. Guests shouldn't be forced to look to the left or right or up or down for too long. I would rather open up a room and spend money on a structural beam or columns than keep a structural wall that cuts off flow.

This is not to say that a bar can't have more than one area designating different purpose and energy levels. Visual layers make a room inviting — as long as people can see the layers and understand them. A game room or area for shooting pool or playing darts can be an asset, and these features definitely increase beverage sales. Separate areas have to be connected visually to the greater public area of the bar. Even people who want to have an intimate talk with a friend want to maintain a psychological or emotional connection to the place they are in. Relegating such activities to back rooms or dark corners makes people feel neglected (even if the service is good) and second class. I lay out a restaurant with the philosophy that everyone wants to sit in an important seat. A corner that looks unattractive has to be treated through décor or lighting to make it more appealing and important. This goes directly back to reactions.

I recommend creating communities, not rooms, within your space. Consolidate games into one space; place intimate as well as community tables to give patrons a choice of how they want to congregate. At the Canyon Inn, we removed a built-in stage that projected too far into the room and replaced it with a portable stage that could be removed to make space for large and small group tables during the off hours.

At Swanky Bubbles, the original bar was split into two levels, with the second floor reserved for private events and to provide relief if the bar became overcrowded. In the downstairs area of what became

Sheer, we created a mix-and-mingle area with medium energy, and upstairs we created a high-energy dance environment — but it would still remain available for the occasional private event. Downstairs we installed a curtain system so guests could control and personalize the degree of privacy they had from their neighbors.

Weber's Place wasted valuable real estate and created a "space vacuum" that made sitting in the main room feel ill at ease. Kervin didn't know how to exploit the stage for additional seating on nights when no bands were booked. Minor and movable alterations turned the platform into additional dining space and a full-time moneymaking area — to the tune of $10,000 a year per chair.

The Bamboo Beach Club and Tiki Bar in Fort Lauderdale generated additional revenue by replacing revenue-neutral lounge chairs lined up around the perimeter of the bar (which no one wanted to lie down on) with comfortable bistro tables that sit up to four people. Each chair has the potential to generate $15,000 annually. What's great about the new setup is that the chairs offer guests a spectacular view of the beach and put the women and men "on a pedestal" — giving passersby a spectacular view of *them*. When men see pretty women lining a bar and vice versa, believe me, they stop in to check out what's going on.

Now I'm going to mix it up a bit because your market also defines comfort. Shiny, hard surfaces convey a fast pace, and this might be comfortable for many demographics. Downtown operations that cater to the guy stopping off for a quick one before catching the 6:15 don't have to install cushy seating that encourages hanging out. An easy-to-navigate, long, polished bar lined with wooden stools and a few booths will do. A swell bar with pillows and an elegant hostess is not what this customer is looking for.

The commuter customer's idea of comfort is a convenient bar with fast service in a stress-free atmosphere. However, once at home, this guy sees himself differently, and therefore his definition of a comfortable bar changes. The local bar in his upscale bedroom community specializes in high-end products like Guinness. In that case, a clubby interior with leather chairs validates the premium price he pays for the beverage — and seduces him to hunker down with friends and order another.

Be aware of overcrowding, even in a bar that has great flow, because most people find packed houses uncomfortable. This has a negative impact upon length of stay and rarely increases revenue. Find the proper fill level — the number of people that makes your place "come alive" without overwhelming your staff or making customers claustrophobic, sweaty, or unsafe. Large crowds can make women especially feel vulnerable or mashed, and that guarantees an early exit. Get head count numbers right by keeping track of how many people are coming and going through the door, and you will maximize revenues. In fact, holding just slightly back on the "perfect number" (i.e., by 5 to 10 percent) actually creates the best sales results in most cases. Never go over the legal capacity of your bar — as an owner or manager, you have to understand that you are responsible for the safety of the people in it.

### *Bar Dynamics*

The energy level and excitement of a bar — what I call its dynamics — comes in great part from the emotional reaction a customer has to what she sees when she walks through your door — and that *should* be the actual bar itself and what's behind it. I believe the back bar — including the selection of premium brands — is one of a bar's most underestimated but dynamic revenue sources. The back bar is your marquee! Don't clutter it up with random items that do not relate to beverage promotions and sales. Think of the bar area as a living, changing space where guests interact with your product and employees.

Furthermore, the bar has to display products to their best advantage — the sparkle and beauty of those bottles should be evident through proper shelving and lighting. At Swanky Bubbles/Sheer, the back and front bar both missed opportunities. The back bar had minimal product organization and display. The front's ugly "artist"-designed bar looked like a brownish marshmallow that had been pulled out of shape by a three-year-old, and it provided a too-narrow work area for bartenders and uncomfortable seating for guests. We tore out the molded foam bar top, which significantly widened the work area. A beautiful walnut cabinet with shelving created a sophisticated and pleasing display for bottles — and appropriate lighting ensured that the bottles weren't lost in the dark.

Lighting bottles from below, through glass risers or shelves, is a particularly flattering way to show off your stock and move the eye to the center attraction. A mirror attached to the back bar increases the power and glamour of up lights and helps reflect the dynamics of beautiful liquor bottles. Spotlighting is effective to highlight taps and top-shelf items. When plotting out where to place shelves and lights, keep in mind the sight line of customers standing or sitting at the bar by standing and sitting at the bar yourself, so you can see what your guests see. Bottle displays on the back bar should be forty-two inches or higher, because if it is lower than that, the customer cannot see them, and you can't sell what's on them.

Choose the liquor brands that will be most visible or front and center carefully and with deliberation. Standouts and featured bottles should be those that are most profitable for the bar. When a bar features twenty-five liquors, placement value decreases.

A unique design element that sets the bar apart from the competition and makes it memorable is another way to energize your bar dynamics. This can be a one-of-a-kind vintage cash register, a unique lighting fixture, wall art, an interactive beverage service station, or a display of unusual proprietary glassware. Obviously any distinctive feature has to be in keeping with your décor or style. At the Abbey in Chicago, my design team created a large chandelier out of a drum kit that, of course, tied directly into the establishment's heritage as a famed music venue. Now the bar, which we renamed the Green Room @ the Abbey, has a very unique and functional feature that makes sense in the context of the bar. People always comment on the chandelier and, again, it adds to the bar dynamic.

At the Blue Frog 22, renamed the Local, I had old photographs of working-class Chicago blown up into large wall murals, which were placed strategically on the walls. Enlarging an image gives it importance and dramatic impact. In this case, the black-and-white historical images make a memorable impression on customers. They are aesthetically arresting—when you are at the bar having a drink and you look at the people in those pictures, you really feel part of something bigger than yourself. At the same time, because you see the people up close because of the image size, the murals create a feeling of intimacy. That creates a powerful dynamic at the bar.

At Piratz/Corporate, we installed a "tap table" visible from the street (there may be some legal issues with these new mechanisms—check with your municipality if old laws are still on the books that have yet to catch up with the latest technology). Customers pay for a key that operates beer taps that are integrated into a table. Each key allows a guest to pour two beers of his choice. This is a very unique feature that gives the bar area a social and interactive dynamic that even passersby can see through the front window—a tremendous draw for new customers. Tap tables also increase length of stay by requiring patrons to prepay for beverages. No one is going to leave before getting that second beer. Naturally, food orders from key holders tend to increase during the time it takes to drink two beers, more so than people who are ordering beer and paying for it one at a time.

Did you know that 70 percent of people entering a room, whether public or private, make a right-hand turn? Place your most enticing feature (the bar, usually) on the right side of the room and make sure it is well lit because that's where your customer is heading. Look at malls—if one has a major entryway, the stores to the right do better business than those on the left.

### *Lighting*

Bar lights, like the lighting in any commercial building or private home, have to function for the people in it. In work areas like the kitchen and the back office, task lighting has to be bright enough for people to do their jobs. At the bar, lighting should show off what you're selling and give the bartender and servers adequate illumination to get their jobs done without it distracting customers or ruining the mood. Because of eye movement and management, nothing should be brighter than the back bar. Those are the simple practical considerations of lighting. It gets a little trickier when designing the public spaces in your bar. Here is some lighting science to keep in mind.

Brightness focuses our attention. Focal points, like the back of a bar or a dance floor in the back of your space, have to be more brightly lit than surrounding areas if you want to draw people toward and into them. Increasing the contrast between the brightness of an object or area and the surrounding space increases the impact of whatever is highlighted. Brightness also leads us where we want them to go. In one classic lighting study, people read directions to get to a room in the back of a building. There were two equidistant ways to get there — a path to the right and a path to the left. We already know that when people walk into a room, most of them take a right turn — so would lighting the paths make a difference to this natural propensity? Yes. When neither path was illuminated, 69 percent of people went to the right, an instinctual reaction. When the path to the left was illuminated, 75 percent of people took the path on the left. We're like moths to a flame — we just want to go where the light is. This is one of the tools I use to fill empty areas in a bar.

Basically, you can control attention and flow patterns with lighting. If you want to sell high-end vodka, then your display of high-end vodka should be more brilliantly illuminated than the displays of brandy or gin. If customers neglect the far corner of your bar, use lighting to feature it, and people will gravitate toward those seats. If you want to ensure people know how to get to the washrooms, light the way — you don't even need arrows pointing them in the right direction if your lighting sends the message clearly enough. Likewise, if you do not want patrons wandering off in a certain direction, don't light the way.

Lighting also helps people feel comfortable while maintaining a sense of privacy. Research shows that while people like to face walls that are illuminated, and are drawn to them, they also do not want to be in the spotlight when dining, watching entertainment, or talking privately or in a group. In studies of lighting and choice, people never choose to face a dark wall or area, and they always show a preference to be adjacent to light areas, not to be directly in them. For a bar, this means that intimate tables should be softly lit and will be even more appealing if the adjoining areas, like a stage, a dance floor, or the back bar, are brighter.

Lighting also conveys value. When a shopper goes into a brightly lit department store, she expects to see lower prices than in a more softly lit boutique or high-end department store. A typical discount department store like Walmart has about a thousand lights—all of them putting out the same flat, task-oriented illumination so people can see the merchandise and the low prices. A more upscale department store like Bergdorf Goodman may have those same thousand lights, but they are much more layered, sculpting areas and highlighting mannequins and other unique items because mood is more of a concern than price. They are going after different consumer emotions. Lighting must always serve a defined purpose beyond its mechanical function.

Likewise, fast-food restaurants are normally brightly lit, while expensive restaurants have lower lights and higher prices. A standard McDonald's is like a beacon to travelers on the road. There is no mistaking that you can get a warm, cheap meal inside. And you'll have no problem reading the menu on the wall above the service counter. When McDonald's opened McCafés and began modernizing and redesigning traditional McDonald's stores, the company changed color palettes, making them more muted, and replaced downscale fiberglass furniture with wooden and metal versions. It also changed the lighting from office-style fluorescents to more residential-style fixtures — but the illumination level didn't change much. McCafés still have to be brightly lit to maintain the idea that the restaurants still offer a family-style bargain. Plus, people still have to see what they're doing when they're using the free Wi-Fi and sipping coffee.

Yet there really is only one function of a McDonald's, and that is to provide cheap food quickly. That message does not necessitate numerous layers of lighting. A more upscale fine dining experience with higher prices serves many emotional needs — not just food, but intimacy, a culinary experience, conversation, and so on. That's why expensive restaurants use more layered strategies to illuminate different areas — the entryway may have a chandelier, while the bar area might use soft spotlights and back bar up lighting, while dining tables may be softly lit with small lamps or miniature ceiling spotlights. A garden or patio seating area might be even more layered, with up lights in plants and string lights providing twinkle but no function.

Many of the bars we rescue have horrendous lighting, mostly because the owner didn't really think about it as part of an overall business strategy. The basic response I hear when talking to bar owners about their badly lit bars is either, "Well, I figured people need to see so we put pot lights in the ceiling," or "People want to be anonymous in the bar so we kept it dark." Both attitudes are wrong. A bar that is too brightly lit lowers length of stay, while a very dark room reduces guest interaction and the overall guest experience.

Lighting helps identify bar mood; a dive bar is going to be lit differently from a sleek, sophisticated sushi and sake bar. Yet no bar can get away with single-source, overall flat lighting. *All* bars need to use layers of lighting from a variety of sources to sell product, control patron flow, enhance comfort, or drive higher prices (a great layered lighting system can get you $2 more per cocktail). Identify what mood you wish to create in your space. If you offer dancing and live music, dynamic light and color keep the energy up on the dance floor. However, some areas of the room should be more muted so that guests can take a break from the action and sit and enjoy a drink. That requires softer colors and lower lighting. If you have a local hangout, choose colors and lighting that support easy eye-to-eye contact among patrons. Light bars softly where patrons sit and more brightly at the back bar to encourage longer conversations but also awareness of what the bar offers.

The lighting and colors at the Chicken Bone looked as though they were pulled from an amusement park. The industrial tile floor was a hodgepodge of clashing colors, and the overhead "intelligent" lighting, which could be set to any color at all, was dumbly dialed to green most of the time. If you want to make people, and especially women, look as unattractive and sallow as possible, light them with green. Ditto for food. Wow. No wonder most patrons stayed at the bar and so few ventured into the dining areas. The color and lighting fixes were pretty straightforward. We installed a dark neutral-colored floor, painted the walls, and reprogrammed the light system to a more flattering and relaxing color.

Both Rocks and the Olive Pit were dark to the point that it wasn't even clear whether they were actually open for business. When people enter a space that's dark, the first thing they think is: "What are they hiding?" In both of these cases, there was plenty to hide — but once we cleaned up and renovated the interiors, the new style demanded showing off. A variety of spotlights, hanging fixtures, up lights, and floor lighting promoted eye movement to and from different-use areas (game playing, dining, drinking) and "sold" certain areas, like the bar itself.

## Music/Entertainment and Sound Quality

As a musician and manager of music venues, I learned the importance of energy and entertainment in increasing guest enjoyment and extending stay. For example, you can see how the same ten songs, played in a different order, provide a completely different experience. Seeing the impact of rhythm, tempo, and music mix had a strong impact on me. As a result, I have the only federal patent ever issued for a system that manages music to achieve a desired impact in hospitality properties. Every aspect of music in a venue impacts sales—not only in bars but in virtually every type of hospitality property as well, including quick-service restaurants, casual dining, fine dining, and hotels. And not enough operators get that.

A weak, poorly designed, or improperly used sound system will greatly shorten your length of stay. Too much bass, improper equalization, too few speakers, and other factors cause strain on guests' eardrums and premature guest fatigue. That means people feel "drained" earlier and leave sooner. If music is not perfectly flowing during the night, fixing it should be a major priority. Even live entertainment can be boring. Never allow more than thirty seconds between songs and make sure live bands keep their energy properly positioned as the evening progresses.

If your bar uses music as a background feature and not as foreground entertainment, choose wisely. It should not be an afterthought, as in the bartender just slips his favorite iPod mix into the speaker system. The Hard Rock Cafe founders would measure customer response to their music program, and over time they discovered that loud, fast music made patrons talk less, consume more, and leave quickly. Because Hard Rock is primarily a dining establishment and not a bar, this technique worked in its favor, because when the chain first opened, in 1971, there would be long lines of people clamoring to get in. Turnover and consumption were keys to the venue's success, at least in the beginning. As the chain became more ubiquitous (there are 175 Hard Rock locations in fifty-three countries), Hard Rock changed its approach to music and now allows more customer participation in choosing music type, volume, and pace.

> Target music to your customer by looking at radio station rating reports in your market, including who listens to which music when. Scarborough Research and Arbitron both provide valuable radio research reports, which can be tailored to your area and customer.

More controlled studies have shown that speed and volume of music affects consumption rates. One study done at Fairfield University in Connecticut found that people ate faster when background music was sped up from 3.83 to 4.4 beats per minute. Nicolas Guéguen, a French behavioral scientist, discovered that beer drinkers consumed more beer when music was played at higher volumes. Specifically, when a bar's music was set at 72 decibels, people ordered an average of 2.6 drinks and took 14.5 minutes to finish one of them. When the volume was turned up to 88 decibels, customers ordered an average of 3.4 drinks and took 11.5 minutes to finish each one.

In the study "Effects of Atmospherics on Revenue Generation in Small Business Restaurants," researcher Jeff Shields found that an increase in music volume led to shorter meal durations and an increase in turnover. Scottish researchers Clare Caldwell and Sally A. Hibbert, both of the University of Strathclyde, also confirmed that slow music increases length of stay, while fast music shortens length of stay. People who dined under the slower-tempo conditions showed almost a 17 percent increase in meal duration over their quicker-tempo counterparts. When I was a consultant for the Rainforest Cafe, management wanted to increase turnover, so the chain experimented with the tempo of its rainstorm feature. Perhaps thunder and rain isn't precisely music, but the same theory applied. When the restaurant ran its storm every eleven minutes instead of every twenty-two minutes, people left the restaurant earlier and more people could be served. It represented millions of dollars of additional sales each year.

Slow tempos increased spending by an overall average of 23 percent more than fast tempos. Caldwell and Hibbert found statistics that are very interesting for bar owners: when spending was broken down into food and drink, food dollars increased 12 percent, while money spent on beverages increased a whopping *51 percent.* The moral of the story: neighborhood, lounge, or intimate bars that use music for ambiance should select slow- to medium-paced music set at a comfortable volume to optimize both length of stay and money spent.

# 7

# Visibility Is Money

> We require from buildings, as from men, two kinds of goodness: first, the doing their practical duty well: then that they be graceful and pleasing in doing it . . .
>
> — JOHN RUSKIN,
> NINETEENTH-CENTURY ENGLISH ART CRITIC

THE FADED EXTERIOR OF CHAMPS, a Burbank, California, institution, was straight out of the 1970s. The very first sports bar in town advertised its achievement poorly — with multiple cheerleader megaphone cutouts tacked around the top perimeter of the building, a marquee that was missing some of its letters, and tired, dated diagonal strips of light-stained wood siding. Even though the bar is located in a great market area — the annual income of residents is $67,000, well above the national average — the exterior sent a sad and discouraging invitation to potential customers. Champs didn't look like a place that had anything to offer a young, sports-oriented patron, and that impression is exactly why most people kept walking or driving by.

Refreshing Champs' exterior included modernizing its signage and logo, losing the megaphone decals, and minimizing the dated diagonal wood siding by painting it black. We added a hand-painted tagline — "Burbank's original sports bar since 1983" — along the front of the building to communicate what was special about the bar compared to the newer, corporate-owned sports bars that had opened nearby in recent years. "The oldest" and "the original" are legitimate selling points — tired and dated are not. In fact, old or vintage elements are fine — as long as they are authentic and an intentional part of your look and concept. Stadium-style lighting ensured that foot and car traffic could spot the bar's updated appearance and reinforced the sports concept. Now people would be encouraged to drop in, curious to see if the interior of the bar was as fresh and inspiring as its new façade.

The Abbey Pub in Chicago, like Champs, held an iconic place in its city, in this case because of its fame as a historic music venue. Yet the outside of the pub was drab and messy — a dirty awning, old music posters, and faded signage sent a powerful if unconscious message to passersby: "Our time has come and gone." It was also difficult to tell where the bar entrance was as opposed to the entrance for live acts. When people do not immediately know where to go to get what they want (music or food and drink in this case), they usually give up and keep going. We cleaned up the Abbey's exterior, washed its awning, replaced messy posters with streamlined guitar imagery that had a purpose, and created a separate entrance for the music section of the building, designating it "the Green Room @ the Abbey," complete with its own sign and well-lit, easily identifiable entrance.

The Black Sheep in Cheviot, Ohio, had a confusing exterior — the large plate-glass window made it look like a retail store. You expected to see a mannequin. Rather than trying to make something that wasn't working work (should we put a big keg in the window?), we opted to make the window go away without actually replacing it. It's expensive to remove a large window and construct a wall in its place. A major structural change would have been onerous and time-consuming in terms of required permits and inspections. It was quicker and cheaper to build a removable (i.e., nonpermanent) enclosure that hid the window. Timber trim on the false front mimicked the look of Tudor architecture, a feature we carried over to the rest of the building's exterior. We reused the bar's existing neon sign but changed the name from the Black Sheep to the Public House. It was now immediately identifiable as a pub, leaving no doubt in passersby's minds that it was a place to sit down and have a drink.

The most depressing exterior so far on *Bar Rescue* has to have been Angels Sports Bar, which I introduced you to in chapter two. A strip club, also called Angels, connects to the bar. The two separate businesses were indistinguishable; both had the same dingy white paneling pockmarked with staples and covered with the remnants of posters for music acts long gone and out-of-date meal specials. Several motorcycles parked out front conveyed a sense of menace. Studies show that motorcycles deter women — and without female customers, you can't have a successful bar. A pit bull tethered to a post further advanced the location's forbidding narrative. No surprise so few of the more than seventeen thousand cars that drove by Angels each day bothered to stop.

Owner Renee Vicary and I took a closer look at the outside of the building. After noting the disgusting condition of the front of the building, we moved out back.

"What's this?" I asked her, nodding toward the jagged, chewed bottom of the employees' entrance.

"Squirrels," said Renee.

"And what about that?" I asked, pointing to a large hole in the blacktop next to the door, adding, "I saw an animal in there."

"Squirrels," Renee repeated.

"Or rats," I suggested, as they were the more likely culprit. Renee told me she didn't want to fill the hole "because there might be babies in there." Babies, I might add, that were infiltrating her kitchen, spreading disease, and violating health laws.

Lack of upkeep sends a very clear message to customers, and that is: "What's dirty and dangerous looking on the outside is going to be even more disgusting and disturbing on the inside." We cleaned up the grounds, patched the holes, repaired the damage to the siding, repainted, and added landscaping to the front of Angels. The most I ever focused on landscaping was with Angels—I put a lot of money into live plants so the bar looked vibrant, new, and cared for. It's a way you can bring your image closest to the street—three colors of bushes, shrubs, and flowers.

We painted the bar side of the building with a new and different color, changed its name to Racks with a pool rack triangle logo, and created new signage to further differentiate it from the neighboring strip joint. No Parking signs placed in front of the building ensured motorcyclists used the rear of the building. Dog owners were politely asked to either keep their canines at home or leash them in the back.

The message a bar sends from the street largely determines who walks through the door. That's why the difference between Angels, the strip club, and the newly anointed Racks Billiards and Bourbon, the adjoining bar, had to be clear *at first glance.* The Black Sheep became the Public House, but changing names alone wouldn't beckon locals through its doors. The venue had to *look* like a pub from the outside, whether or not a customer noticed its name above the door. Patrons at Champs understood the visual codes of its old exterior (crappy, outdated, no fun, old-fashioned), which is why few ventured inside. The new visual cues at Champs said, "We're historic, but relevant" — energizing the neighborhood to take a second look.

## Put On a Good Front

There's a reason why *Bar Rescue* "reveals" take place outside. We want management and employees to experience the same first reaction their business will have on the community. Our exterior makeovers are public statements: "We're back, we're better, and we want to prove it to you." First impressions count, whether you're trying to convince people to give a new place a go, remind them of a previous pleasant experience, or persuade them that you've changed the negatives inside. An unkempt, ill-maintained, or run-down façade attracts an equivalent customer. A well-lit exterior with curb appeal makes women and couples feel confident that something worthwhile and safe awaits them inside.

In focus groups and other market research, women say over and over again that bar and nightclub parking lots are not bright enough, and that landscaping that looks like people could be hiding in the bushes are deterrents. If you want women to come to your bar, never underestimate the power and appeal of a safe, brightly lit parking lot and a manicured landscape that does not offer hiding places. When I supply these features to a failing bar, I can double its female head count within three weeks.

Hell, even middle-aged bikers and blue-collar beer drinkers need visual indications that assure them they can nurse their tasty drinks in peace. Dive bars need visual charm that tells locals and adventurous bar hoppers, "This is a bar with lots of character and cold beer," not "This is a joint where you'll get in a knife fight." Otherwise you risk losing an entire demographic of people who love to experience the gritty realism of a truly great dive every once in a while. Consider Manhattan's Subway Inn on East Sixtieth Street. Small neon "bar" signs flank the main sign above the door; the front window is ablaze with light signage for various beers, the Mets, and an ATM. Its old double French doors are painted black. This place couldn't scream "Dive!" any louder if it tried. The bar's cheesy but inviting façade is one of the reasons the Subway Inn has managed to, so far, hold its own with regulars (some of whom, legend has it, haven't left their barstools since the place opened in 1937), locals, and curious first-timers alike — despite the appearance of many more polished places in the neighborhood.

The exterior of Weber's, on the other hand, worked against the bar. An oddly tall roofline and dark-painted front walls made Weber's look shady and ominous, exactly like the cheap strip club it once was. It didn't matter one bit that the word "bar" was on its new sign, or that it was advertised and marketed as a music venue. From the street, Weber's registered as weirdly nefarious and grubby. Like many snippets and remnants of information, strip club "signifiers" live deep in our unconscious, memories of things we might have seen before, either in a movie, on TV, or in real life. Taffer team experts had the same reaction I did when looking at Weber's for the first time, and without knowing anything about the building's previous occupants: "Looks like a strip club." Our reactions speak directly to the power appearance has to influence our perceptions. After we covered Weber's roof with gray, weather-beaten shingles, the fairly inexpensive fix transformed a liability into an asset. Now the bar looks like a friendly island beach shack instead of a quasi-dangerous strip joint.

There are times when obfuscation can work to a bar's or restaurant's advantage, specifically in large metropolitan areas where foodies and trend seekers are on a constant hunt for the next hot spot. In very crowded marketplaces, the counterintuitive strategy of hiding can be a competitive asset—the more obscure the better. Hudson Clearwater in New York's West Village is officially located at 447 Hudson Street. Its entrance, a graffiti-covered unmarked green door, is actually around the corner on Morton Street. There are numerous similar "secret" bars in other cities, like the Varnish in Los Angeles and Vin De Syrah in San Diego.

Those who go the invisible route better have something extraordinary inside that promotes word of mouth, press review, or other media coverage. These three establishments all earned excellent reputations for food and drink. But in order to earn those good grades, *someone* had to find these places and then like the experience enough to spread the word, along with their secret locations. Unmarked bars and restaurants still have to market themselves through influencers in the community. It has to be a true destination, because they will not get spontaneous customers. Let me also say successful hidden bars are exceptions that prove the rule that *your* bar should have an identifiable door, façade, and sign.

The fact is, in most cases, a bland or invisible exterior is economic suicide. In most situations and communities, if you are invisible you are meaningless. The Olive Pit was completely concealed behind a strip mall, and there was no signage or any other indication of its existence visible from the busy boulevard out front. The circa 1962 blue-collar watering hole located just thirty miles southeast of Los Angeles had begun a downward slide as longtime regulars fell away and weren't replaced by new customers who might have given the bar a chance had they known it existed. We eventually changed that, along with other problems that plagued the bar. But difficult or obscure locations are not an excuse for failure. When I rent a space in a mall, whether it's enclosed or an exposed strip mall, investing $200,000 to get noticed doesn't make me flinch. Visibility is a priority when you do not have the built-in "eyeballs" that a well-traveled thoroughfare or Main Street location offers. I have to communicate my message and move the customer's eye toward my door. Getting noticed doesn't always come cheap.

Here's one of my most memorable examples of the power of an exterior: A forty-year-old, upper-end Dallas restaurant was in dire need of a face-lift. The family's next generation, two brothers, realized this and had taken over with the intention of remodeling and then repositioning the restaurant for a new generation. They brought me on to lead the project, and we made the decision to remodel and revamp the menu while remaining open. The outside of the building was covered in dated white stucco that once signified a European or Continental look—that had to change.

We hired a painting contractor who used a special Pepto-Bismol-pink primer before applying the final color. The day after the primer was applied, it started to rain and didn't stop for more than three weeks straight; the contractors had to wait nearly a month before they could apply the final color. During the restaurant's "pink period," revenue increased by more than 200 percent. People would come in and tell us that they had driven past the building for twenty years, but they had never "seen it" before. Once the building had become *highly* visible, albeit hideous, guest counts and sales increased without one other marketing effort or even a completed renovation in place. Since then, I've never looked at the exterior of any business in the same way.

Rocks, a smoking bar in California, was located in an industrial park and looked every bit the part. In fact, locals used to refer to the place as "the dive off the five," and that was not meant as a compliment. When we transformed Rocks into Power Plant nightclub, the new theme was industrial and techie. It was an idea we wanted to convey dramatically at the entryway, which originally was just a forgettable metal door. We created a large metal awning that gave dimensionality to the entrance. A smoke machine operated by the doorman every half hour or so created billows of steam around the door, again creating dimension. We added tall columns of real flame lights to flank the front door. Basically, I took a piece-of-shit entryway and made it very cool and meaningful. It looked as if it had been placed in an industrial park on purpose.

## Build Smart

Before you change the exterior of a business, consider its purpose, market objectives, and financial goals. Structural or even cosmetic changes should never be done for purely aesthetic reasons. There are three aspects of building: good, fast, and cheap — but you can usually only get two at a time. If you want something good and fast, it ain't going to be cheap. If you want something fast and cheap — forget about quality. See what I mean? Decide what you want — you can get two out of the three. Of course there are exceptions, but not very often. Obviously, bars have to look good, but appearance must follow function, not the other way around. Spend money on exterior enhancements only if they are necessary to comply with building codes, create beneficial customer reactions, and support financial targets. Get noticed!

> If customers have to step up to get into your space, foot traffic drops almost 50 percent. There are exceptions to this rule, so know your audience. Clothing retailer Hollister consciously uses outside steps in conjunction with other unconventional strategies to appeal to its young demographic. Stairs may also have a positive correlation to a bar targeted to college kids. However, in most cases, it's worth eliminating steps if possible or minimizing their negative impact. Widening a step up, for instance, makes it appear lower and less like a level change.

To put this in perspective, consider that renovating an existing property from top to bottom, inside and out, can run from $70 to $300 per square foot, or more, depending on the finishes you choose. Building an average bar from the ground up using standard construction materials for the core structure or shell alone costs between $100 and $120 per square foot. It costs another $100 to $300 (or more) per square foot to install interior fittings. That could add up to about $250,000 to rehab an average-sized 2,200-square-foot neighborhood pub or $250,000 to $500,000 (or more) to build a bar from scratch. We spend on average between $150,000 and $250,000 on each *Bar Rescue* rehab.

These budget numbers may sound substantial, but money gets eaten up very quickly if we need to repair or replace plumbing, exhaust systems, furniture, bar tops, flooring, and other finishes. During the rescue of J.A. Murphy's in Fells Point, Maryland, we had to replace the defunct refrigeration and plumbing systems and eradicate an extensive vermin problem and its associated filth. That wasn't all: We had the unexpected task of rebuilding the floor when my designer, Nancy Hadley, discovered a rotting support beam underpinning the building — the result of a total disregard the owners had for known plumbing leaks. We had to evacuate the building and make sure it was structurally sound before opening. That required getting the city involved, hiring structural engineers, and bringing in a construction crew of several men. We had to put in twenty-two floor joists across the entire span of the building as well as new footings. It cost more than $40,000. Poof! There goes the money. Is it any wonder we renamed the bar Murphy's Law?

At any rate, only about 20 to 25 percent of our rescue budgets go toward refreshing or rehabbing exteriors. This has to include major problems like those at Murphy's Law (which admittedly blew past the normal allocation), as well as "minor" or noninvasive modifications such as painting, light construction, general repairs, new lighting, better landscaping, and custom signage. During the Black Sheep/Public House rescue, we reused the original neon sign and limited the exterior treatment to a simple application of timber trim. I asked my designer to find a way to hide the confusing storefront window with a partition wall, which would not incur the substantially higher cost of demolition and construction. A simple box made from standard, off-the-shelf building materials covered the window and can be easily removed if necessary. The basic building project dramatically improved the bar's curb appeal, but the changes were also a deliberate part of the experiential and revenue strategies to market the Public House as a cozy pub.

No matter how light or heavy your exterior's redo, you may be able to save a great deal of money by hiring a company that does residential additions and renovations. On average, commercial contractors cost 30 percent more than these residential remodeling professionals. However, residential contractors are only useful for smaller neighborhood bars. Large spaces, or those located in strip malls, substantial retail developments, or urban areas, require a commercial contractor. If you have your eye on becoming the impresario of a ten-thousand-square-foot dance and party nightclub, be prepared to comply with city inspectors and work with union crews. Plan on opening your doors about $1 million in debt — *before* you've hired a staff, bought inventory, and marketed the place.

## Give Them a Sign

There are many wonderful ways to enhance a building and get noticed, and I'll deal with those shortly. Before the lighting and flags and planters and benches, however, is the sign. The shout-out to your customer, your bar's sign should contain a memorable message that is unique and contains a strong and recognizable graphic element that is scalable for a variety of uses — on menus, advertisements, calendars, websites, social media sites, T-shirts, or other promotional material. People see, interpret, and understand visual language before they understand or even register written words. I believe the world is moving toward iconography, not to the abandonment of words, but as a more inclusive and immediate form of communication that more people — *more customers* — can embrace. Walt Disney understood this. He said, "Of all our inventions . . . pictures still speak the most universally understood language."

Get your sign and its iconography right and it will serve you well for many years. Just because I love science, I ran across an interesting study that shows how brand logos penetrate our consciousness. Social scientists had previously believed that brand iconography was language only children older than five understood, but T. Bettina Cornwell, a professor of marketing and sports management at the University of Michigan, and Anna R. McAlister, a lecturer at the University of Wisconsin, found that three- and four-year-olds can easily identify which logos corresponded with which brands.

This recognition wasn't limited to obvious candidates like Disney and McDonald's (93 percent of children could identify the golden arches), but also "adult" brands like Toyota (recognized by 80 percent of kids) and Shell (recognized by 50 percent of toddlers), a finding that surprised researchers. It doesn't surprise me a bit — great symbols elicit predictable and recurring responses. *Associations were strongest when the toddlers connected the image to a positive past experience.* That is an important finding for bar owners to keep in mind, because let's face it, we're not all that different from toddlers when it comes to connecting the dots between a great experience and a symbol of that experience. We do it all the time. See golden arches: think French fries. Spot the orange and pink pillow letters of a Dunkin' Donuts sign, and you've got coffee and donuts on the brain. There is no need to actually read the script of a Ruth's Chris Steak House sign — the sight of the logo's round "U.S. Prime" meat stamp and bold red "Chris" is enough to elicit memories of a thick, juicy steak.

T.G.I. Friday's red-and-white-striped street sign logo is not only internationally recognizable; it stands for food and fun. The stripes are crucial for the brand, especially as it moves into both familiar and foreign markets. I was the keynote at the Friday's 2012 annual meeting at the Gaylord Texan Resort and Convention Center in Grapevine, Texas, and the entire convention center had been recarpeted in those red and white stripes. There was no doubt in anyone's mind that Friday's was in town. It was a compelling reminder of the importance of graphic branding. When you do it well, it becomes a vital element of a brand.

It would be an amazing accomplishment to create a sign and logo that registers with your customers the same ways national brands insinuate themselves into our unconscious. I try to create a unified name and logo for clients, including those on *Bar Rescue.* This is a place where I recommend spending a few dollars and working with a designer who has experience with restaurant and bar logos. The art, logo, typeface, and color have to complement what the bar's positioning is trying to achieve.

One of my favorite signs was the one we did for Win, Place or Show, which became America Live, a bar with a focus on live music. We incorporated the top neck of a guitar into the name, and there was no doubt what the bar was about. It was memorable, scalable, and, like Walt Disney said, universally understood. We transformed a run-down Irish bar on Redondo Beach into a surfer bar called Breakwall, incorporating a simple blue surfboard graphic into the sign. It was bold, visible from a distance, and immediately recognizable for what it was. At Murphy's Law, we created a sign that included the *M* on one side in a box attached to the larger sign — conveying the idea that the designer forgot to make enough room for the entire word. On the other side of the sign, the *a* and the *w* from "Law" were placed in the box. Even though the sign and logo used only words, it was a graphic representation of a common mistake familiar to most of us. It said this is a bar that's fun, quirky, unusual, and unexpected. Most important of all, the sign was memorable.

Sheer, the former Swanky Bubbles, incorporated a simplified floral lace design and the name into a diamond-shaped logo that, had the owners not changed the bar back to its original name and subsequently failed, would have stood the test of time. It was scalable — it worked on business cards, the menu, staff T-shirts, baseball caps, and large-scale posters. It was the perfect iconography for a bar with a mission to attract women but not turn off men.

Make a list of words that you associate with the business — these help your designer pinpoint shapes, mood, and tones. What images come to mind when you think about a whiskey bar or a casual hangout famous for its local brews? A wine bar? Modern, slender lettering or iconography that speaks to vineyards, grapes, bottles, or corkscrews is a starting point. Do a few renderings and ask your target customers what they think. You know who you want coming through the door — it's not that difficult to gather these people together and solicit opinions.

Friends aren't necessarily reliable barometers of what works and what doesn't because honesty is a touchy subject. Your friends' friends are good candidates if they suit your target demographic. If someone says, "Oh, it looks expensive," and you're not going for expensive, you need to tweak the design. If nine out of ten people react negatively to the color, find out why. I'm not convinced social media is a cure-all for business, but it is a useful tool for collecting consumer reactions and opinions. Post your logo on these sites, ask for reactions, and look for similar comments. A good designer will work with you until you're happy and pronounce the project final.

Once you have a great sign and logo, use it everywhere you can.

Signage can be hung over a door or attached above it. Decals can be placed on street-facing windows and transfers can be applied to chalkboards that sit on the sidewalk to advertise specials or entertainment. The idea is to get the name and logo into your customers' and community's psyche.

Many locations can't add signage because of city codes or the expense. Don't be deterred. Most municipalities can't control what you put on your windows, so decals are a must—but they don't attract customers until they've tripped over your place. In one *Bar Rescue* episode, we had a situation where we couldn't put an actual sign on the building. I had a transparency of the logo made that could be projected on the side of the Public House (the former Black Sheep)—it had to have been thirty feet high. Very few laws legislate light. Of course, you have to ask the landlord if you don't own the building, and the lighting effect only works in the evening, but it's a heck of a lot better than having no sign at all. And, in fact, projected signs make an impressive statement.

If lighted signage isn't an option, you have to get creative. Most cities and towns can't prohibit someone standing on the corner wearing a sandwich board since this activity is usually covered under free speech law. A bar that was still waiting for its sign to be delivered was ready to open, so I parked a line of cars right in front of it and put simple copies of the sign on the cars' windshields with arrows pointing toward the doorway. Or I will make logo sun visors and put them in employee cars parked in the front. You may not be able to do that every night, but if you're launching a new business, be bold, and do whatever it takes to be noticed. In many cases the solution becomes more fun and unexpected than a conventional sign.

## Gold Is in the Details

Angry Ham's looked like a big white metal box (actually, it is a big white metal box) and was often mistaken for an industrial warehouse or an auto body shop. Nothing about it said come on in for a cold beer and a burger. There was no time to rebuild or change the structure of the building — we had to work with what we had. Whatever we did would have to be immediately recognizable as "restaurant" to moving targets (i.e., customers in cars, since the venue is located near a busy highway).

We tapped local industrial sculptor and welder Stretch to design and build a sixteen-foot three-dimensional metal sculpture of a brunette outfitted in snug mechanic's clothes holding a tray with a pizza and drinks. She was installed right next to the bar's elevated pole sign. Drivers couldn't miss her. Stretch fabricated two oversized pieces of silverware that were attached to the façade of the building and could also be seen from a distance. There is no longer any confusion about what Angry Ham's offers, and both the giant lady and the utensils reinforce the overall point of view of the bar: larger than life, fun, and substantial.

The design elements didn't technically change the building, but they had a dramatic effect on the bar's exterior — they added easily understood iconographic information to a building that offered few options for change. We're forced to work with what we have on *Bar Rescue* because the show's thirty-six-hour turnaround simply doesn't leave time for the luxury of massive construction. Even without time limitations, I wouldn't recommend that an independent bar owner tear off the front of a building and start over.

There are numerous ways to enhance a building and provide relevant information with a minimal amount of construction. Outdoor lighting is an economical and effective way to show off attractive architectural features and downplay other less appealing aspects of a building, to direct customers to entryways and parking lots, and to provide a sense of warmth and security. Champs used stadium lighting for its practical and symbolic effects. The three-dimensional entryway of Power Plant sent an important message. I've used spotlights to highlight signs and patio dining, floodlights to create "red carpet moments," strobe lights to create movement outside a nightclub, and string or "fairy" lights to illuminate landscaping and set a romantic mood.

Bench seating in the front of a bar is an invitation to hang out when there's nice weather and conveys the idea that your bar is fun, social, and active. Flags or banners create movement and catch the eye. Place flags on your property's perimeter, building edge, or roofline to increase visibility; they benefit sales every time. Visually, flags and fabric banners can be designed to complement many venues, from sports bars and beer gardens to local hangouts, beach bars, and other casual settings.

Flags are not appropriate for every venue, of course. You would never use flags to call attention to a luxury cocktail lounge. However, I have to say that people who run expensive establishments make the mistake of thinking that blending in is somehow dignified or expected. This is just nonsense. Management and owners who believe in this strategy are foolish. Even the most expensive restaurant must make itself known—in fact, of all places, bars that offer expensive liquor and food need to be noticed the most because they have huge operational costs to cover, which include the demands of reaching a smaller, niche market.

"Sticking out" does not mean forfeiting your image in exchange for inappropriate exterior marketing. Feinstein's at the Loews Regency Hotel in New York City—one of the premier cabaret venues on the East Coast—uses burgundy-and-white awnings printed with its name over the club's street-level windows to distinguish itself from the hotel it calls home (another clever idea if hanging a sign is out of the question). You can't miss it, but no one would ever think Feinstein's was compromising its integrity or clashing with the refined tastes of its clientele. Large planters full of lush foliage and flowers or topiary are another elegant way to flank the entryway of an upscale cocktail lounge. Add up lights to create drama at night; it's still in keeping with a sophisticated atmosphere. In fact, such techniques reinforce the idea of refinement and style. Trees also add height and architecture where none would exist otherwise.

Setting up barriers or rope lines on a Wednesday night (for instance) drives traffic, even if no one is standing on line. Red velvet rope makes people curious—what's going on inside? You'd be surprised how many people want to find out. I've done crazier things—like placing freestanding PARKING RESERVED FOR DEREK JETER signs at the space right by the front door. Was the baseball great expected? Of course not—but it captured the interest of enough people to make that opening a success. I've also used "positive picketing" effectively to generate interest. Employees carry "protest" signs—which say things like PRICES TOO LOW, DRINKS TOO DELICIOUS, BEER TOO PERFECTLY POURED, or SERVICE TOO GOOD—and walk in circles around the front of the building. It's fun, it engages staffers, and it energizes passersby.

This is a tough business climate—costs are high and consumers are price resistant. There is no time to hide your assets under a rock. This is clearly not the time to be shy. Your building is your calling card. What else can you do physically to look relevant and appealing? That is the goal of exterior design and marketing. Remember — if you are invisible, you're not creating reactions.

# 8

# The Revenue Response

Rule No. 1: Never lose money.
Rule No. 2: Never forget Rule No. 1.

— WARREN BUFFETT,
US ENTREPRENEUR AND FINANCIER

WHEN THE BLACK SHEEP BAR AND GRILL opened its doors in 2007, the Cheviot, Ohio, local hangout took off—raking in about $70,000 a month in sales even though there had never been a particularly disciplined financial strategy in place. Over time, owners Scott Scherpenberg, his uncle Tommy, and his cousin Greg, seduced by their initial good luck, became distracted by other responsibilities—Scott is a firefighter and his co-owners have other jobs and commitments as well. Inattentiveness because of these competing demands eventually led to a series of predictable woes: staffing issues, deterioration of standards, customer dissatisfaction, and declining sales.

Like many of the intervention subjects on *Bar Rescue,* the Black Sheep's problems were compounded by loans meant to minimize the impact of falling revenues until business magically—because there was no turnaround plan—improved. It was only a matter of time before the partners' neglect and ill-conceived (that is, nonexistent) financial strategies caught up with them. By early 2012, the bar was losing $8,000 a month and had accumulated more than $700,000 in debt, a liability that Scott's two partners knew nothing about because he'd borrowed the money without telling them.

When I met with Scott, Tommy, and Greg, I could see they were sincere, hardworking guys—they were motivated to save the bar and willing to accept the fact that they'd have to change their behavior and recommit to maintaining high standards. Sure, the restaurant needed some updating and a good cleaning. But the central issue was a complete misunderstanding of how to budget, track, and control finances. These three were desperately in need of some revamped business planning, a serious budget based on actual data, a realistic plan to get out of debt, and new controls that would start putting more financial figures in the plus column.

## Revenue and Reason

The root cause of financial issues that many bars (like the Black Sheep), restaurants, and other entrepreneurial businesses face is the wrong mind-set. If you don't have the right attitude for the job, you will never do the job well. Here's the problem: too many people open bars because they love bars. Of course I've heard the adage "Do what you love, the money will follow," but I don't buy completely into it, at least in this industry. Your greatest shot at success in the bar business comes because you love *business*. If you're not passionate about digging into the numerous accounting, tracking, inventory, and data analysis aspects of running a bar, you're just going to hang out all day and lose all of your money. I've seen it happen.

Bar owners fall into two categories: the social owner and the business-oriented owner. Trouble is, not many people are good at combining both traits. Of course, social skills benefit customers and employees, but management acumen is also a must. These two qualities can often feel contradictory to many passionate and gregarious entrepreneurs. Understood. It's not easy being everyone's best friend while also maintaining authority, reading reports, and commanding the respect of staff. It's wise to remember, however, that you are *not* opening a bar (or any business) for your own amusement. You are opening it to serve your customers and to make money. If you don't think you can handle both sides of the task well, I recommend finding a business partner who complements your strengths — either a hands-on person who can work the front of the house, or a backroom pro who thinks building algorithms is fun.

Like a lot of the owners I meet on *Bar Rescue,* Scott and his cousin and uncle were definitely in the social corner. They weren't drinking their own product, giving freebies to friends, or allowing workers to goof off during shifts like the people over at Angry Ham's. However, they didn't *run* the bar either — being physically present doesn't constitute management. Lack of motivation was due in part to the fact that all three had other jobs — the bar was an enjoyable pastime that over time had become a burden. What do we do when we're tired and yet another obligation vies for our attention? We avoid it. Bingo. Until these partners accepted that the bar needed real management, they'd remain in a financial hole.

If the Black Sheep were to survive, it had to build up and maintain a cash reserve, set a realistic budget, and manage both. Today my budget projections are spot-on; one of the aspects of my consulting business is helping owners and management determine cost and revenue estimates, whether it's a start-up or an existing property. But it wasn't always the case — a few failures early in my career provided valuable insight into the importance of proper planning. In 1992, I opened the Alamo Grill in the Mall of America in Bloomington, Minnesota, and within three months I was in the hole for $400,000. The Alamo actually had unbelievable sales, but it still bled cash because I didn't have the right cost structures in place before opening. This was at the center of one of the most powerful lessons I learned about finance.

As a young, cocky know-it-all, I thought I didn't need a detailed opening plan, a contingency plan, an accounting system, cash reserves, or an appropriate line of credit. Between overruns on construction and the expense of promoting and opening the place, I had no cash reserves to cover the constant costs. Getting things in and out of the building was a nightmare. There were more than 450 stores and restaurants all being built at the same time in the same building, each with different contractors. There were times when we had to wait an entire day to access a freight elevator during the construction period. How could I have predicted any of this? When I opened, I was already over budget and did not have positive cash flow after two months, even though I was doing great business. We were so busy that my food and beverage overhead remained high. By the time I needed those plans and systems, there was no time to put them in place because the restaurant was so swamped.

An incredibly successful property that was constantly packed in what is still a very popular and heavily trafficked location . . . and I was out of money. That situation forced me to find a partner and give him 60 percent of the business for $200,000 to get me over a tough financial hump. The following year we did $800,000 in profits on over $3 million in sales. Had I conserved more capital and controlled costs from the beginning, I would have reaped the benefits of that accomplishment. I wound up selling the restaurant for well over $1 million a few years later, but that "deal with the devil" forced me to give away 60 percent of the profits. I never made the same mistake again.

Since then, my first order of business when opening a bar or restaurant is to focus on costs, customers, capital, and expenses. In fact, I'm a nutcase about research, including detailed demographic, psychographic, and competitive analysis. There are nine data groups I work on before I make even one decision about a business. I take a marketing conclusion and I turn it into an objective. I turn the objective into a strategy, and then I work on what kinds of tactics can help reach the goal I've set. By the time I get to that point, it's been several weeks. There is no room for gut decisions in my business; my clients' livelihoods are on the line. I will not allow an operation to open without a budget. So if you're afraid to look at numbers, get out now while you still can. Otherwise, make friends with your calculator and spreadsheet program. You're going to need them.

## The Perils of Not Planning

Consider this: more than half of every dollar you make is already accounted for even before you open for business. Don't believe me because you're under the impression that "liquor is 80 percent profit"?

Here's how it all breaks down. Occupancy costs can't exceed 10 percent of total revenue. If it does, you are taking money directly off the top of your profits. That means rent, taxes, and any other fixed elements in your lease or mortgage have to stay at or below 10 percent of sales. If you spend 15 percent on occupancy costs and don't budget correctly, you screw yourself before you've even poured a beer. Beverage costs can't exceed 21 percent of beverage revenue, food shouldn't surpass 30 percent of food revenue, and labor must stay below 28 percent of total sales.

Lack of adequate capital to sustain operations through crucial start-up months or temporary economic downturns is another reason businesses suffer. Even if you've been smart about pricing and cost controls and you're meeting percentages, you *still* need cash reserves to maintain standards, staff, and inventory if and when you hit a rough patch. This reminds me of a story about a customer who ordered a taco salad in a Brooklyn neighborhood restaurant:

The entrée arrived and it looked at first glance as if it were generously sprinkled with shreds of cheese. On closer inspection, it was clear that shredded carrots, not cheese, covered the salad. The customer called the waitress over to ask why the taco salad had no cheese, a typical ingredient of every taco salad she'd ever eaten. The server hesitated and then excused herself to check with the chef. Returning to the table, the waitress nervously told the guest, "The chef doesn't make his taco salad with cheese." Actually, the chef was struggling to survive; he had no cash reserves and was out of inventory, including cheese, and couldn't afford to send someone to the local grocery store to pick up an emergency block of cheddar. Two weeks later the place closed.

In order to figure out where you fall in terms of expenses, calculate one-time costs (building, equipment, recruitment, furniture, website design), ongoing costs (product, labor, utilities, web maintenance), and marketing costs (advertising, flyers, cards, coupons), dividing the total into either twenty-six or fifty-two weeks. Use this figure to calculate what kind of sales you need to make every week to break even or make a profit in sixty to ninety days, or up to a year. In general, a neighborhood bar customer spends on average $14 to $18 every time he walks through the door. Upscale or other special concept bars and nightclubs can run significantly higher per customer.

Play it safe and bank on losing money for some extended period of time. Overnight successes happen, but they're rare, so don't make being an instant sensation a part of your budgeting. The number of months and the amount of cash you need varies by the size and location of your business, the kind of audience it appeals to, and the product it serves. Some high-end, high-cost businesses open up with a projected loss in the first year. Smaller businesses might safely project a break-even or moneymaking point within sixty to ninety days.

If you're opening a new place, you need to settle on an opening budget, or what it will cost to launch the business, because you can't just open your doors and expect people to wander in off the street. Opening or launching requires advertising, marketing, special signage, and/or loss leaders (deals on certain food or drinks that you intentionally lose money on to get people in the door). Once you've got that piece of the puzzle figured out, take 25 percent of the opening budget figure and put it aside for contingency. Anything from a delay in getting permits issued to major global, national, regional, or local events may force you to pay rent without any business to offset those costs.

I had a grand opening of a new nightclub called Palmer's in suburban Chicago. On the afternoon of the opening, the Gulf War, Operation Desert Storm, began. No one came out. Everyone stayed home, glued to the news. Not for one evening, but for weeks. It was very destructive—we had staffed the business, marketed the business. I'd spent all my marketing money for the planned opening. Had I built the Taj Mahal and put Jimi Hendrix inside, I would have had the same problem. Nothing I could have prepared for could have made a difference in this event—no average citizen had any clue that on August 2, 1990, the nation would go to war. Whatever you plan for, make sure your contingency covers something worse. Breaking news about catastrophic events, political scandals, weather disasters . . . these are incidents you have no control over. A traditional contingency is 20 percent of your worst-case scenario. Palmer's had the contingency funds in place to weather the early days of Desert Storm. Contingencies are not for controllable elements of your business; they are for that which is out of your control. One thing you can bank on? Predict the unpredictable.

If you do manage to pull off a grand opening on schedule and on budget—congratulations! Your contingency cash still comes in handy when market conditions change or an emergency situation comes up for any reason. Even the most experienced owners make mistakes: they discover that their customer base or neighborhood is somewhat different from what their data indicated, costs rise, or facilities get damages—all of which can have a negative effect on revenue until proper adjustments can be made. What happens if the price of your commodity goes up? In 2012, the price of chicken wings went up 25 to 50 percent. In today's economy, there is no elasticity in pricing, so it's very hard. You can't just double the price of chicken wings; you have to raise prices across the board. The contingency fund can cover higher costs until the change in prices puts you back on track.

## The Double Secret to Managing Revenue Results

When people manage bars by revenue alone, they screw up. Once up and running, many owners and managers judge success on sales alone. Wrong. If you're just looking at sales or revenue, and you're not doing guest counts, you really do not have an accurate picture of market share or whether your business is growing. Always manage by guest counts and sales per guest. It's the only way you can accurately gauge sales and revenue.

Say one hundred people come in this Friday and you make $1,000 in sales. Next Friday, you make $1,050 — gee, sales went up! But without doing a guest count, you don't know that you only had ninety customers who spent a little more. And here you are, thinking your business grew when in fact you lost 10 percent of guest count. The following week, 110 patrons come in, but sales were only $900. If you don't look at guest counts, you would think sales went down. You really didn't have a guest count problem that week; you had a sales problem. But you don't know this unless you are relating revenue to sales based on guest counts.

When you know your guest count, you have a better idea of how the business it doing and can identify whether you have a sales, guest count, or staffing problem, and the right solution becomes more apparent. If it stays the same or goes up, business is doing well, your promotions are working, and you're creating the right customer reactions. If guest count is up and sales are down, what went wrong with sales? What caused you to do fewer sales with more people? Was the bar packed and fewer people were served, or were they served less? Were servers trying to look after twenty-five or thirty people or more? Impossible.

Say you have five tables of four people per server. That means she needs six minutes to take an order, bring it to the bar, and deliver the drinks. The server has to repeat this procedure for each of the remaining four tables. That means the server won't go back to the first table for twenty-four minutes. The server can't handle more than twenty people — some of her customers are already feeling the pinch in service. There are empty glasses at some tables, and at least one table hasn't seen a service person for more than twenty minutes. If the ratio is higher than twenty people per server, sales per guest goes down, and that has nothing to do with guest counts or promotions. It is a staffing problem. You better add another server.

> A major breakfast chain tried to pump up its stock price by saying its sales went up by 4 percent, when it had really increased prices by 7 percent. So actually, the business did not grow at all; it shrunk. The restaurant lost 3 percent of its guest count.

I do not let guest counts trend down for more than a week. Looking at head counts during peak hours and slow times tells you where you need to invest in more staff. Guest tracking also makes it easier to recognize whether you have a marketing, sales, or customer transaction or reaction problems. Asking guests if it's a first time or repeat visit is a must. Do people come in never to return because they didn't enjoy the experience? You can only tell after you have collected and aggregated enough data. Or is traffic simply slow and spotty — do you average fifteen guests at lunch when you estimated twenty-five or thirty? These are two different problems that must be corrected in two different ways. Pinpoint the aspect of a customer experience that isn't working, and you can change it and salvage the numbers. If it's food, adjust the menu. If it's service, work with the staff on improvements or recruit better people. If you aren't getting the traffic you anticipated, make changes to marketing, advertising, and first-time customer offers.

## Under Controls

The success or failure of a bar is, of course, a combination of many factors, but a major contributing factor to revenue shortfalls can often be attributed to mismanagement of the big three cost centers — labor, beverage, and food. Over- or understaffing shifts either wastes manpower or places unnecessary stresses on available resources. Employee theft and careless and constant over-pouring sends money down the drain; inadequate management of perishable inventory leads to expensive waste. Owners and managers have to eliminate theft, establish pouring protocols, manage inventory, and set prices that are profitable and suitable for the marketplace.

Corporate operators are fortunate to have advanced electronic systems that track labor needs and costs, monitor inventory, prevent theft, and flag prices when they lag behind rising food and beverage costs. Yet even the most sophisticated automated mechanics don't let managers off the hook. *Management must manage.* And while state-of-the-art systems are extremely helpful in gathering and coordinating information, they're also expensive. Independent and regional owners and managers can't always afford to install POS (point-of-sale) hardware, for instance, and continue to struggle with containing labor, food, and beverage costs. Yet thousands of bars flourished before the computer was even invented, and the same straightforward steps and tactics these bars used to maintain their edge still work to keep critical controls in line.

### *Labor Is Easy!*

Manpower is typically the most expensive component of any business. Therefore, if you can contain or reduce labor costs even by a few percentage points, it represents big bucks in profitability. The good news is that payroll is really the easiest of the big three to manage if you dedicate time to tracking and managing it as a percentage of your total sales.

The typical mid-priced restaurant runs at a labor cost of approximately 30 percent of total revenue. A bar or nightclub can operate at a considerably lower percentage, about 18 to 24 percent of revenue, based upon the type of venue it is — dive bar, cocktail bar, beer and sports pub, and so on. For example, if you knew your sales were going to be $1,000 tomorrow, you can easily cap labor spending at $250 or 25 percent. In other words, the total costs of all your shift schedules together cannot exceed $250. Every bar spends its total labor budget differently as needed, allocating among the kitchen staff, bartenders, servers, security, and other employees. Typically, about 60 percent of the total labor budget is allocated for the back of the house (kitchen, maintenance, administrative) and 35 to 40 percent for the front of the house (servers and other revenue-generating employees). However, this is not a hard-and-fast rule and the split may be different in your operation.

The trick to consistent labor cost tracking and management is forecasting shifts accurately. Forecast revenue each week by the day *before you create schedules* so you can determine exactly how much you have to spend on labor before the fact. If a forecast is too low, you won't have enough staff to fulfill expected sales—the result is fewer sales and more frustrated customers. If your forecast is too high, too many employees will be standing around doing nothing while you're going over labor budget. By monitoring actual traffic results every day and comparing them to your forecast, you'll know right away if and when you went over budget.

As soon as you identify when labor costs have gone off the rails, adjust them by reducing employee hours for the rest of the week or month, sending employees home early, or eliminating slow shifts and lengthening the remaining shifts to ensure continual coverage. These simple modifications get you back in line within days. Forecasting gets easier and more accurate after a couple of weeks of diligent tracking. Once you master forecasting sales, monitoring results, and adjusting as needed, you hit your labor cost target every time.

### *Beverages Are Basic*

Never forget that in a bar, liquid is gold. Drinks are always the main moneymakers. It comes down to simple mathematics: the cost of producing a drink is far less than the cost of producing food in terms of both labor involved and ingredients. As a general rule, 21¢ of every beverage dollar generated goes toward product cost. This number is an average calculated from a bar's typical sales mix. If beverage costs surpass 21 percent of beverage sales, something is very wrong. Manage your costs within the following parameters:

- **Typical** spirits and mixed cocktail cost is about 15 to 17 percent.
- **Typical** bottled beer cost is about 23 to 25 percent.
- **Typical** draft beer cost is 21 to 22 percent.
- **Typical** wine cost is about 30 percent.
- **Typical** soft drink cost is 6 to 8 percent.

Now come standards. Again. Without standards, it is impossible to forecast costs. Furthermore, a bartender can pour any brand and amount he chooses without breaking any rules. You can't blame employees if they find themselves operating without guidelines. At the Bamboo Beach Club and Tiki Bar, the bartenders were beautiful and blond, but lack of mixology rules meant drink prep lacked consistency. Customers never quite knew what they were getting. Sometimes the ladies would over-pour; other times they used call or premium vodka without an up charge. Weber's Place was worse—the head bartender didn't have any recipes or basic bartending skills; he didn't have a clue. Bye-bye money.

The standard quantity of alcohol in a cocktail is 1.5 ounces per drink.

Cost containment of consumables begins with consistent recipes and uniform procedures. It is impossible to manage and track the cost of a martini if the ratio of vermouth to vodka or gin, total ounces of liquid, and preferred type and size olive are unknowns. Every cocktail, no matter how basic, must have established ingredients in set quantities that include exact specifications for ingredients, pour quantities, and up charges related to name brand requests. This is the only way you can set prices based on facts, not fantasy. Now you're on your way to manageable costs and inventory control.

Beer can be a cash cow for many bars, but without standardized pouring criteria, product loss is a huge and expensive problem. Pouring beer into a glass so it's half foam — that *one* misstep — can increase costs by 20 percent! In order to solve the problem of foamy beer at the Canyon Inn in Yorba Linda, California, owner Pauly Ambrus implemented a "save the foam" campaign instead of instituting and then teaching the proper pouring technique to the staff. When a bartender served draft beer, the huge head of foam was poured into another glass and stashed in a cooler beneath the bar until it settled, after which it was served to an unsuspecting customer. This is not the way to preserve the integrity of product — or customer traffic.

Bartenders and other servers must master proper and accurate pour techniques, learn the proper glassware for various drinks, and adhere to recipe specifications. These should be nonnegotiable standards. If you have an electronic or automated tap system, test and maintain it on a monthly basis to ensure optimum pours. Correct bartender (or anyone's) errors when you see them. These management tasks will absolutely lower your costs. Controls and standards serve customers' interests too — no guest will ever be surprised by a subpar product or one that doesn't taste just like it did last week. That sidecar, cosmo, or tap brew will be as tasty each and every time.

### *Stay on Par*

Maintaining correct inventory levels is essential to controlling costs and maximizing profit potential. Have what you need on hand and you fulfill the promise your menu makes to customers. At the failed bar Swanky Bubbles in Philadelphia, the owners neglected to maintain liquor inventory; as a result, bartenders were unable to make many cocktails on the menu. Food inventory management also reduces waste — raw chicken wings or tomatoes go bad if you have more than you need. Even frozen foods deteriorate if they are held too long. Inventory is managed by establishing correct order amounts using a system of "par levels," a hospitality term that indicates the quantity of liquor, food, and supplies an establishment should have on hand between deliveries.

Bartenders must keep tabs on how many bottles of each spirit are used each week, just as a cook tracks how much food rolls out of the kitchen. If you use eight to ten bottles of white rum and twelve to fifteen bottles of citrus vodka each week, the par for white rum is ten bottles and the par for citrus vodka is fifteen. You may not use all of these spirits every single week, but using the higher number as your default par level ensures you won't run out of profitable products. If the kitchen uses twenty pounds of ground beef every week, twenty pounds of meat should be in the fridge at all times. Orders should reflect the par level minus what you have on hand. If ten pounds of ground beef is in the fridge on order day, order ten pounds. If you have four bottles of white rum in stock, order six more.

### *Great Food Doesn't Have to Be Fancy or Expensive*

The price of food is considerably higher than the price of beverages, and the margins on drinks are wider than those of food. Food sold in bars is rarely more than 30 percent of total revenues. To put this in perspective, the food/beverage ratio at restaurants is flipped. Friday's,

Chili's, and Applebee's run about 17 to 20 percent revenue from beverage sales and 83 percent of revenue from food sales. They would all love to pop that 20 percent on beverage revenue, but it's very hard to do for a restaurant. Bars don't want more food sales — the profit is in the drinks, as I said. That's why it's a waste of money for most bars to hire highly trained chefs.

An experienced cook — one who can competently turn out simple menu items, store and work with fresh products, keep the prep and cook areas clean, and maintain efficient output — is all you need. Unfortunately, most bars I rescue have food costs close to 50 percent — way too high to sustain over the long run — because they do not have a precise food program or the right person overseeing and managing the kitchen (and its stock) efficiently. What really struck me about the Black Sheep's financial difficulties is how they could have been minimized with proper controls and pricing. The pub's hamburgers, for example, cost $1.20 *more* than they were sold for. Every time a customer ordered one, the owners lost $1.20 because of bad pricing.

There are three basic bar menus: convenience (as in, while you're here, you'll have a little something), destination (e.g., Belgium fries; "Irish nachos"), and experiential (e.g., having a theme; being a quiet place to eat and talk; being romantic; showcasing sports; providing environmental changes). What is the point of your menu? None of these concepts require overcomplicated menus. A really great burger goes a long way; likewise, something special but straightforward like hand-cut sweet potato fries, assorted fried pickles, or Cajun popcorn shrimp can entice customers to linger a bit longer and order another cocktail.

Develop a repertoire and a reputation for doing two or three dishes really well. This is where a bar can blow it with food. Make everything else basic, familiar fare that can be easily, consistently, and well prepared. Boy meets girl — the most erotic thing you can do is share food, so on a couples-oriented menu, food that is easy to share, like appetizers for two, enhances that interaction. For convenience dining, nothing on the menu should take more than ten to twelve minutes to make. A destination food program has to pay attention to plate presentation.

Consistency in food is a standard that, like cocktails, is achieved through recipes that specify exact ingredients, acceptable substitutions, and quantities per serving. Every good bar or restaurant has a photo of every plate hanging in the kitchen as a reference for cooks to maintain consistency in presentation. Unless the cook knows what he is supposed to put on a plate, he may pile the equivalent of two servings of French fries on one order and half a serving on another. He may make one burger with four ounces of meat and another with six. How can you set a fair price or manage guest expectations? How would you feel if you got a big burger one day and a much smaller one the next? More important, all food recipes must be strictly followed or your budgeted costs will be of no help in forecasting inventory needs and restocking schedules. Your cook and prep staff must stick to recipes, quantities, and specifications absolutely, no exceptions.

Kitchen staff must be taught to have respect for products, recipes, and efficiencies. Food that is overprepped or mishandled can spoil and make customers sick. To control waste, you have to take a proactive role. That means regularly inspecting the pantry and walk-in fridge to ensure proper temperatures and storage, and checking garbage pails for wasted food. Don't want to? Sorry, that's what it takes to succeed in the bar business.

When restocking inventory, keep a close eye on vendor prices. If your recipes are priced for a particular cost percentage and ingredient prices go up, your cost to produce the item increases, which means you have to raise your prices if you want to stay profitable and within percentage goals. Work closely with your suppliers, but never give them the impression that you won't go elsewhere for a better price. Cross-bid every consumable product *every month;* whoever has the best price should get your business. Competitors will work harder to get your business next time with aggressive pricing.

### *Theft: The Second-Oldest Profession*

Theft is still a major and troublesome issue in our industry — it's simply a fact of life in businesses that rely on cash transactions. There are many ways a bartender can steal. At Weber's Place, one employee simply took full bottles of liquor for his friends. Since there was no inventory control at the bar — too many people had access to the liquor room — the missing stock wasn't even noticed. Once we limited access and fired the thieving staffer, that stealing stopped. Unfortunately, after we left the thief was rehired, and I can't tell you whether there's still a secure lock on the storage cabinet. Oh well.

A more common and insidious scam is, for example, when a bartender delivers two drinks to a customer and charges twenty dollars (drinks are ten apiece). The guest gives the bartender a twenty. The bartender rings up a ten-dollar sale and puts the twenty in the cash register. A little while later, the bartender "remembers" that the drawer "owes" him ten dollars. He does this five times during the evening, so now the drawer "owes" him fifty bucks. Suddenly he "runs out of singles" in the cash register and uses the tip cup to make change. He takes ten one-dollar bills from the tip cup, puts them in the cash register drawer, and then slips out three twenty-dollar bills and drops them in the tip cup. Now fifty dollars is in the possession of the bartender. The same cycle occurs the next night, and the night after that. From a distance or to an inexperienced owner, everything looks just fine.

Some dishonest bartenders use pennies, matches, paper clips, or other small objects near the cash register to keep track of his "overage" due to under-ringing, because if the thief loses count he is exposed . . . the jig is up. Never tell a bartender what he owes you in sales because he will count that amount of money out and keep the rest. Conversely, if he does not know the sales number and counts the money, he might just be over $20 — you've probably got a thief on your hand if that happens more than a couple of times, because no one is over by that much "by mistake." An overage might happen once by mistake, but if it happens twice, you've got a thief who can't count. Hitting "no sale" is another trick to get extra cash from under-ringing, but I can see how many no-sale rings are done, and if it's more than two times per night, don't try to tell me you're making change — it's theft.

Bartenders and servers can never be allowed to make transactions between the tip cup and the cash register. Write this rule down and set it in stone as a way of ensuring managers and supervisors adhere to it. Track how much is being spent on liquor by using a company like Bevintel. Company reps weigh every liquor bottle in your place and then compare it against the register. If your register or POS system says you sold 100 ounces of Tanqueray gin on a given night and the Bevintel measures say 120 ounces were consumed, you need to figure out where that 20 ounces of Tanqueray went. Sometimes you'll find that a bartender's friend likes that brand of gin — when there is an abnormality there's generally a good reason for it.

Pour cost analyzes the relationship between cost and sales. If a bartender serves a drink and pockets a portion of the proceeds, he's increasing cost without increasing sales, and the pour cost rises. However, if the bartender *replaces* the stolen half ounce of liquor with an equal amount of water or iced tea (depending on the spirit), pour cost looks legit, but the drink is weaker than it should be and the guest is "robbed."

**Well** drinks are poured "out of the well," a "speed rack" of stock liquors kept at the bartender's station. Well liquors are often used to make basic mixed drinks such as a rum and Coke or a whiskey sour. These are the most affordable drinks for the bar and the customer. **Call** drinks are those made from specific brands "called" by the customer, who might order something like "Smirnoff and orange juice" or "Jose Cuervo Gold on the rocks." Bars can and always should charge more for drinks made with call liquors. **Premium** drinks are those that use top-shelf brands like Ketel One, Bushmills Black Bush, Crown Royal, or Bulleit Bourbon. Super-premium brands featured in some upscale operations include VSOP cognacs, thirty-year-old scotch, and so on. These are the most expensive drinks a customer can buy — and the most expensive bottles a bar buys.

Under-pouring is yet another technique bartenders use to steal. The bartender pours a series of four drinks using 1.25 ounces of liquor apiece instead of the standard 1.5 ounces. The difference in the quantity is not detectable by the consumer. That means the bartender has an ounce of liquor leftover and unaccounted for. He sells a 1-ounce shot of liquor to a customer for cash, and that money goes right into the bartender's pocket. This has zero effect on pour cost.

If you think there's something fishy going on behind the bar, look very carefully at sales. This is all part of your tracking. Bar productivity is a measure of bartender sales per hour. It is computed by dividing the shift's gross sales by the number of hours the bartender worked. To calculate the staff's productivity, total the bar's gross sales and divide them by the total bartenders' payroll hours for the week.

Calculate day and evening shifts separately because for most bars there is a big difference between day and evening receipts. Two night bartenders might ring up $7,860 worth of sales in the week and clocked in a combined 75 payroll hours for $104.80 per hour. The daytime guy might do $2,654 is sales over 38 hours for $69.84 per hour. Keep track of productivity per hour for each shift. After six or eight weeks, you will see patterns — not only will this reveal your best sellers behind the bar, you will also see who might be falling behind on a regular basis.

So how do you know if he's stealing or just a subpar bartender, especially if you cannot be on the premises all the time? "Secret shoppers" can "spec" your service and pinpoint potential or existing issues. Many professionals and chains use these services; for $50 you can hire a couple to visit your bar and give you a review of staff, food, drink, and service. These "customers" can also provide some insight into the honesty of workers, as they are very attuned to the signs and signals of theft. Post reviews where employees can see them as a very effective motivator.

Of course, it all comes back to engaging and managing. Watch how the bartender works: Is he slow or unfriendly? Is he following recipes or producing lousy drinks that don't inspire second rounds? If it turns out that the bartender is just not keeping up or meeting the standards you have set for service, personal dynamics, or quality of product, move on and find someone who will. Even though this person isn't stealing per se, he's costing you money. If he's operating quickly and personably, but the receipts don't make sense, you could have a thief on your hands. Thieving bartenders are often extremely charming people. You may have to send in reconnaissance—I do it all the time. A friend who is not known at the bar goes in and orders a call drink. You can check receipts to see if it was rung up properly. Likewise, you can check quantities and shot sales. There's always a way to catch a thief.

> Do not give more than two trusted people keys to liquor and wine storage, and maintain a strict tracking system of what bottles leave the room. I have found bottles of premium liquor filled with water in more bars than I like to think about. It's unfortunate, but it's also a fact of life in the bar business.

Kitchen theft is not much different from bar theft. Years ago, I was the manager of a large chain of bar-restaurants in Florida and I had a pretty serious food problem—missing steaks. I knew what my food-to-guest counts were because this chain butchered its own steaks on the premises (I can still butcher a butt with the best of them). One day I decided to quietly observe activity on the loading dock from a few hundred yards away. I was going to figure out where these expensive steaks were going if it killed me. Some food thieves put inventory in a bag, leave it on the loading dock, and then pick it up when they leave. But I didn't see anything like that on the platform. A couple of dish machine operators (DMOs) were out there awkwardly moving around, so I decided to walk over and see what was up. One DMO was wearing a ball cap and I noticed some blood dripping down his forehead. I lifted up his hat and there they were: two unwrapped strip steaks sitting on top of his head.

Was he evil? No. Was he a thief? Yes. However, it is my job not to give people an opportunity to steal or to excuse it and thereby condone the activity. That's why I had to fire someone who was trying to feed his family. Honestly, it's a terrible position to be in; it stinks. You have to take responsibility, but I still feel bad for the thief because taking food is different from taking money. I get the difference, but it doesn't mean I can forget about it and give the guy a pass. It broke my heart to let him go because, while the thieving bartender really was the devil, the steak thief was bringing food home to his kids. But it was up to me to eliminate the conditions that make stealing food so tempting. That's on me. Keeping honest people honest is my responsibility. I had to put tighter product-tracking controls in place and eliminate temptation. Management *must* stay close to product movement throughout the day or night so unusual changes are noticeable. Don't make thieves out of otherwise nice people through lax inventory controls.

## Price Is Perception

Slapping an arbitrary value on menu and bar items ignores a key component of the business we exercise complete control over. Basing prices on real data means you can charge and receive *the most* for your products even in a tough economy. Pricing food and drinks properly and profitably at the Black Sheep, for example, was crucial in stopping some of its money bleed. Food should not cost money to serve.

A lot of owners and managers are nervous about crossing a line where a number becomes unacceptable to a customer. The economic climate has many bars and restaurants decreasing profit margins instead of raising prices. It's understandable but it's a mistake. I'm sure you've seen significant shifts in how customers order and spend—giving away the store is not the appropriate response to this situation. The shift in consumer spending habits provides an opportunity—not to lower prices but to offer greater value. As consumers "reassess," they look for goods and services that they perceive provide "more for their dollar." We use the term "value" too broadly. "Absolute value" is a simple price comparison, whereas "perceived value" is the result of your quality, experience, and business dynamics. Pricing has a great deal to do with perceived value.

The businessperson who is told by customers that his prices are too high usually shouldn't believe it. When people show price resistance, what they are really saying is that the experience you're providing is not worth its price. Guests don't leave a great restaurant or bar experience and say it was expensive. Price is only an issue when a customer doesn't have a positive reaction to an experience. Guests leave marginal or disappointing experiences feeling ripped off. Successful fine dining and up-market operations prove that every day.

The whole point of perceived value is selling to customer desire, ego, and fantasy. How many people spend their last dime on something they cannot afford? It boggles the mind how powerful perception is, and in the bar business it is even more so. If you are in a marketplace that accepts a $22 hamburger, you'd better come up with a burger that is worthy of that price.

I took over a nightclub in Los Angeles not that long ago. The prices were moderate, relatively speaking, but a large customer survey revealed that many guests still thought the prices were too high. Over the course of ten weeks, I upgraded the entertainment, staff dynamics, products, and other operational elements of the business. It didn't require a major financial investment, but it made a major impact. By the time we were through, the nightclub was at capacity every night. Okay, time to raise prices—and significantly, about 25 percent—in three increments over several weeks.

After sixteen weeks we had reached the 25 percent price increase, and we were still filled. I conducted a second guest survey. The responses were overwhelmingly positive and virtually *none* included comments about the cost of food or drink. Perceived value—a *reaction*—beats absolute value every time. Those of you who "dig in" and accept the current environment as long term and aggressively learn how to change your pricing and value approaches can *thrive* (not just survive).

Okay, now on to the nuts and bolts of setting prices. While there are times when you offer a loss leader, everything else you sell should make a profit. That means no matter how much ingredients cost, drinks and food have to be priced to account for those costs, plus the costs of labor, preparation, and overhead, not to mention the perceived value your experience provides the customer, the competitions' pricing, and your market's expectations. An ideal beverage price should be five times the cost of making the beverage. That means if the ingredients (liquor, mix, garnish) cost $1.20 to make a whiskey sour consisting of 1.5 ounces of whiskey, 3 ounces of sweet and sour, and an orange slice, then the drink should be priced at a minimum of $6, but preferably more.

That might not be the end of the story, however. No matter what type of bar you open, there's competition vying for the same customer. The exact *science* of pricing is in covering costs and making a profit; the *art* of pricing is finding the sweet spot, the magic number that suits the experience you offer and meets the expectations of your market. You have to look at who your competitors are, and these can include bars like yours, bars within the general proximity of your bar, nearby restaurants that serve similar food or drink or that have a similar ambiance, and bars that are a bit outside of your target neighborhood but offer a similar experience. Look at the menus to construct a competitor price range, from high to low. If a high-end cocktail lounge down the street sells martinis for $15, the local dive bar charges $5, and a popular restaurant catering to a similar customer charges $6.50, then your $6 martini is priced incorrectly. If you have a mid-market bar, you can probably charge anywhere from $7 to $9 for your drink.

Food cost, as I said earlier, should be 30 percent or less than the price you charge. If a 5-ounce hamburger on a poppy seed bun with .5 ounce of lettuce, 1 ounce of cheddar cheese, 1 tomato slice, and 2 slices of red onion costs $2.20, the hamburger should be priced at a minimum of $6.60. But that's a terrible price. The minimum price should be $6.95 because the consumer's perception (or mental calculation) is $6 (I talk more about the psychology of menus and pricing in the appendix). Why leave 40¢ on the table? The competition also plays a role in setting food prices. Say the lowest price for a similar burger is $5.95 at the dive bar, $9.95 at the popular restaurant, and $21 at the pricey place downtown. In the first place, I would never give a food item a whole number price, even if it seems more high-end to do so. That restaurant is losing 95¢ on every burger sale. Like

I said, perception is everything. At any rate, your hamburger could be reasonably priced at $8.95. If a side of hand-cut fries adds $1 to the cost, add $3 to the price. You would still be offering both absolute and perceived value.

There's money in these procedures and systems; they double your profits with surprisingly little effort. But even with great up-to-the-minute information, effective cost control only succeeds when management is engaged.

# 9

# Innovation and the Risk of Wrong Reactions

Work on your business, not in your business.

— MICHAEL E. GERBER, AUTHOR OF *THE E-MYTH*

ROCKS IN LAGUNA NIGUEL, CALIFORNIA, was no longer relevant to the more than one hundred thousand drinking-age students from six colleges that surround the area. The bar attracted none of them, especially females (the fuel that makes a bar run), because it had devolved into a hangout for a group of scary-looking tattooed and pierced members of a drinking gang headed up and encouraged by one of its house bartenders. If you've never heard of a drinking club, the purpose of membership is to meet and get completely blotto. That's it. It almost makes a drug gang seem useful.

The once-popular dance club had fallen out of favor after it lost its unique feature, smoking, when the loophole in California law that allowed patrons to light up inside the bar was closed. Most businesses have to continually adapt to entice new customers and prevent regulars from losing interest and moving on. We all remember what AOL used to be. Montgomery Ward, Pan Am, and Prodigy—these companies had successful runs but were somehow unable to continue satisfying consumers. Look at how Apple has changed the world, yet Microsoft is still selling Windows.

Rocks owner Scott Terheggen was simply unable to change how the bar appealed to young people after it was forced to change its smoking policy. The law was no excuse—laws and regulations change all the time, and customer tastes change and evolve over time as well. Nothing stays the same. Scott used the smoking law as a crutch to avoid doing the hard work on the business of his business. To stay relevant, bars, like all businesses, have to pay attention to and respond to regulatory and cultural shifts. This rarely entails reinventing the wheel or scrapping everything and starting over. It does mean honestly assessing your strengths and asking: How can I use what I know to keep my business relevant? How can I update what I offer? What can I give to customers that will make them sit up and take notice again?

In the case of Rocks, it wasn't just smoking that patrons liked about the place—although that false belief had become a self-fulfilling prophecy. When the bar did attract a youthful crowd—and it did for many of the sixteen years it had been in business—a majority of the patrons were on the dance floor, having a great time to the beats of contemporary music. Why couldn't it thrive again as a dance club, but without smoking? In fact, smoking is not really an issue for most college kids. Between 1993 and 1997, the number of US college students who smoked cigarettes increased from 22 percent to 28 percent, according to a study from the Harvard School of Public Health—meaning about 72 percent of college kids didn't light up. After that the percentage stabilized, and a 2008 report from the

American Lung Association showed showed that smoking had declined among college students to 19.2 percent, the lowest percentage since 1980. This means that today, about 80 percent of college kids don't smoke. There were one hundred thousand local college kids in Rocks' immediate vicinity. Rocks had to stop blaming its shortcomings on no-smoking laws. Scott should have changed the bar *before* smoking laws changed. He should have seen that those days were numbered.

We reinvigorated the bar by giving it a dance club vibe, updating its look (after a thorough cleaning, of course), dance floor, and technology. Bar owners walk a fine line when it comes to innovation; it's high risk to veer away from known strengths. Yet maintaining too much status quo doesn't increase perceived value. At Rocks, my first order of business was ridding the nightclub of the drinking gang that threatened its existence, requiring members to remove their gang clothing before coming near the place. We gave the place a new name, Power Plant, to erase the negative connection with the gang members. That's not innovation, of course, just smart business.

Next, since the nightclub was located in an industrial park, we played up that vibe with industrial décor inside and out. But we really "innovated" the dance club idea. We installed state-of-the-art DJ equipment, moved the DJ front and center, and modernized and reconfigured the interior to promote customer interaction. We revamped the drink menu with college classics (shooters and slammers, for example) and added a professional lighting and effects system that created illuminated "laser confetti" on the dance floor. Basically, we took an enduring form of entertainment and made it current. That's the kind of innovation I like.

## To Know You Is to Love You

My job is to minimize risk and maximize profit, which is why innovation makes me nervous. As a professional consultant, someone who has owned a lot of businesses, and president of the largest bar and nightclub trade show in the country, I know that you cannot educate a market to accept innovations with which it has no familiarity. The more out of the mainstream a trend, the higher its risk. This is why I have never recommended opening a mermaid bar to anyone starting out. Does the expense of putting in an enormous water tank so girls in mono-fins can swim around in front of guests sound like a wise investment? Only if you're in Las Vegas. If you're chasing a trend, forget about it — you will never make it in time. You'll suffer from customers looking at you and thinking, "Been there, done that." Trendy bars are just that: they survive until the next trend. Classic bars last forever — as long as they stay relevant. Play to your strengths and existing categories to lower risk and avoid the huge marketing investment necessary to change behavior.

Innovation in the hospitality business is best when done working outward from your successes and strengths, not by walking away from them. I do not favor innovation over listening to customers; I favor innovation *while* listening. It's not that I'm against new ideas, but as a businessman, I need it to protect and maximize investments. An innovation that steps far outside of most people's envelope of expectation can reduce or narrow your market when your aim should be to constantly expand your market. Quirky, weird ideas may work in large urban centers where niche audiences might be big enough to sustain you for a time, but you always have to be prepared to move on. Beginners, and even more experienced entrepreneurs, are better off taking proven elements and innovating around them. I take exception to the idea that new is always better and stand-alone innovation leads the way. You have to innovate based on what worked in the past and do it within your expertise and comfort zone.

Great restaurants and bars teach us so much about how to innovate. Consider this: the oldest restaurant in any city is a steak house. The second oldest is usually a fish restaurant. There's nothing inherently revolutionary about steak or fish — yet these kinds of establishments have lasting appeal. Of course, to compete they have to stay relevant, and the most successful steak and fish restaurants do it by innovating within the genre. In fact, some of the hippest restaurants today are steak houses — traditional can be exciting when it is reignited.

Wolfgang Puck's CUT is a huge success. There is a connection we have with steak — a reaction. How do you *not* connect to steak? Reinvent what steak means and you can grow the audience through the product itself. STK, a steak house in the meatpacking district of Manhattan and in Las Vegas, is a perfect example. There is a DJ in the middle of the restaurant and he plays loud, hip, fast-paced music. It's got to be the highest-energy steak house in the world. Other steak houses tend to play soft background music. STK probably has the youngest and most female demographic of any steak house in the country. The restaurant managed to break down the barriers of the steak house as an über-masculine clubhouse by creating a sexy ambience and atmosphere that attracts women — including mega-watt stars like Cameron Diaz and Beyoncé. It also houses a very trendy bar, Tenjune, that further challenges the stuffy reputation of steak houses and appeals to a young, mixed crowd. But at the end of the day, the restaurant still sells steak.

Burger chain Smashburger understands "inside-the-box" innovation. The burger industry had been starving for innovation and Smashburger responded by combining fast service and affordable prices with a fine dining approach to handcrafting food. Every hamburger is made to order using an unusual technique of "smashing" freshly made ground beef patties onto the grill. It also creates "local burgers" unique to each of its regional locations. You can only get the Twin Cities burger in Minneapolis — that's a burger with spreadable cheddar and aged Swiss cheese, grilled onions, lettuce, tomato, and mayonnaise on a toasted onion bun. And you're going to have to go to Michigan if you want to order its Michigan Olive burger, a patty smothered with chopped Spanish olives, American cheese, lettuce, tomato, and mayo and served on an egg bun. These innovations have been profitable. The privately held company's 2011 sales reached $115.7 million, a 72 percent increase over its 2010 sales, according to its own disclosure to analysts.

When Boston bartending legend Jackson Cannon opened the city's Hawthorne with a partner, it was immediately met with critical acclaim and a spot on many 2012 best new bar lists. The lounge features an eighteen-seat bar; a large, communal high-top table; and cushy lounge seating with a residential vibe. But it might be the bar's interpretation of what Cannon has already proved people like: really well made cocktails and classic bar food with a twist, made with fresh, unique ingredients. A tightly edited roster of special cocktails changes daily and complements a larger menu of classics and original drinks. Cannon understands how to carry the guest experience from handcrafted drinks to the physical experience of being in the bar.

"Once you establish that all the extra effort in crafting a great drink is for a person's enjoyment, why would you stop at the drink as the beginning and end of their experience?" Cannon told *Nightclub & Bar*, an industry trade publication published by the NCB. "How you are greeted, served water and talked through choices all require attention and devotion to be done with real intention and the guests' pleasure in mind. Likewise, the comfort of a seat, the touch of marble, choice of glassware for each beverage and all the details that flow and repeat through service are equal to good recipes, solid technique and quality ingredients."

The Hawthorne bartenders still squeeze fresh juice and make syrups, but they no longer make bitters because there are so many good ones on the market to choose from. The bar's "pantry" menu offers small bites inspired by unique artisanal products from around the world, including a honey vinegar from California and a small-production Sicilian rose-petal jam that's a customer favorite. Tiny fresh-baked soft pretzels with bourbon mustard, house-made petite coffee éclairs, mini Reuben toasts, and fingerling potato skins filled with nutty raclette cheese, bacon, and horseradish cream are as much of a draw as the bar's unusual, fresh cocktails. Take the "Phil Collins," a mixture of cucumber vodka, lime juice, simple syrup, yellow chartreuse, and a dash of cranberry bitters, or the "Dutch Oven," made with Barrel Aged Bols Genever, two sugar cubes, three dashes of Regan's Orange Bitters, and soda water.

Innovation doesn't even have to go as far as Hawthorne's focus on ingredients from independent manufacturers. At the "new" Angry Ham's, we maintained its macho, bigger-than-life image and played off it by giving an unexpected twist to familiar bar food classics. We put French fries in a large round vessel and layered fries with cheese and bacon to create a molten mountain of goodness. We created pizzas the size of small Volkswagens and built oversized "Ham's burgers." Pizza and ground beef patties suddenly seemed new and original. At the struggling Win, Place or Show/America Live, I worked with my chef, Aaron McCargo, to create a menu that gave customers a choice of the major four styles of barbecue: Carolina, Mississippi Delta, Memphis, and Texas. At the Blue Frog 22/the Local, we based our concept around beer and burgers. There's nothing special about that combo, but by offering hundreds of beers and numerous creative burgers, we gave the bar a distinctive edge. The reaction was wild—customers loved it.

> Time marches on. New generations of drinkers demand different experiences than previous generations. Millennials, born in the 1980s and the 1990s, will have all reached the legal drinking age by 2021. Those who have already become "legal" have already had a huge impact on bar service. According to market research, Millennials are more willing to try new drinks—including small-batch craft beer, unusual flavor profiles, cocktails made with boutique spirits, and sweeter-tasting drinks—and accompanying bar food. They're also attracted to organic and sustainable spirits and "hard" beverages of all kinds.

## Ideas with Lasting Value

When you come right down to it, innovation is your obligation to keep your business in step with its market. It's called working *on* your business once in a while, not just *in* it. I advise every owner or manager to devote a certain amount of time each week to keeping up with the marketplace and the industry and how it relates to your specific business. Knowing the birth and life cycle of trends comes from research, reading trade publications and websites, and checking out competitors. Never make up your mind whether you love or hate a new idea, nor project a trend's staying power, without doing some homework; otherwise, you will be caught off guard. Balance what your competitors are doing (who might be fools or geniuses) with what other market indicators are telling you.

That said, there are a few shifts in the bar and hospitality industry that I do think are going to be around for a while, so pay attention to them as you think about the aspects of your bar that you want to change.

### *Technology*

Next-level pour systems are already helping bars account for every drop of alcohol poured. Wireless systems will send pour information right from the spout of a bottle to a central computer or POS system. These are innovations worth investing in. They pay for themselves very quickly.

Electronic menus are just starting to emerge, and as the technology advances and becomes more affordable, they will become more common. In terms of customer service and revenue, e-menus streamline the efficiency of an order as it travels from guest to server to kitchen and back to the guest as a final product. E-menus also show promise in terms of raising average sales per customer, essentially because it's so easy for a customer to "click" his way to a larger and more expensive order. Most e-tablet devices integrate with POS systems; make promoting specials across multiple platforms easier by plugging into social-networking sites and customer messaging systems.

Advancements in interactive systems that engage guest participation will continue to expand. Now customers can personalize and create their own soda flavors with special machines that offer an infinite number of flavor combinations. This technology will change the soft drink service industry. Self-service beer taps, like the one I installed at Piratz, will become more commonplace as Prohibition-era liquor laws are revamped and bars discover the advantages of prepaid beverages. Customers love having control over the bar experience. A new technology, targeted sound, means that I can send specific sounds to individual tables. That means one party can listen to a game while you and your spouse are listening to jazz. Phone payments now interact with POS systems, making paying and tipping easier and more convenient.

"Draft" cocktail machines or "cocktails on tap," which serves mixed drinks automatically, have proven to be a boon for bars that find it difficult to train and retain a consistent bartending staff. However, there are still hurdles some bars and local municipalities will face with this innovation. For instance, the New York City liquor authority temporarily shut down the Gin Palace in July 2012 for serving draft cocktails. According to news reports, the action was based on a Prohibition-era law that forbids a bar from pouring alcohol from its original container into another, then serving it. The rule was created to protect patrons from unscrupulous barkeeps who might water down or otherwise alter their liquor. With change come challenges. This too shall pass.

Personal technology will continue to have a huge impact on customer behavior. Smartphones allow customers to quickly find a place to drink and shows them the way with GPS technology. Smart bars are those that are wired into apps that connect them to their customers and communities. Likewise, smartphone trivia, sports, and word games will continue to evolve — high-tech game playing has already changed how people entertain themselves and interact with others at bars. Expect this to continue to grow — welcome it!

> One thing that will never change is the importance of women to the bar industry. Not only is it impossible to survive as a bar without a robust female customer base — unless you are running a "gentleman's club" — women also hold tremendous sway when it comes to selecting a place for a mixed couple or group to eat or drink. *Make sure your place holds some appeal for women.*

### *Democracy in Action*

In order to survive and attract an enthusiastic constituency, all bars will have to offer the added value of friendly, unpretentious hospitality. People have a lot of choice in how they spend their hard-earned money — why should they give it to anyone who treats them like crap. This is great news for civilization! Snobby mixologists who look down on guests and intimidate them will give way to well-trained bartenders who also have great "barside" manner. You can teach a person your recipes, but you can't teach someone how to serve a drink with style or to develop a winning personality. That means you'll need to spend more time hiring bartenders for their personal dynamics: Are they crazy about bartending and love learning about new spirits and cocktails? Do they like teaching guests about what they know? Do they smile, and are they outgoing? Do they enjoy chatting up guests? Do they know how to make customers feel valuable? If so, you will reap the rewards of both repeat and word-of-mouth business.

Related to this shift will be a move toward less complicated drinks that are accessible and delicious. That doesn't mean fresh ingredients and high-quality spirits will go out of style, of course. Instead, mixologists will no longer create cocktails with complex ingredients meant to intimidate the uninitiated, and will focus on new cocktails and classics that embrace the curious! Shot cocktails, vodka-based drinks, frozen concoctions, and classics like martinis and rum and Cokes will live very comfortably alongside whatever new combos turn up in the shaker. Bartenders should enthusiastically welcome whatever a guest wants to drink and make him feel good about his order. No guest should ever be looked down upon for ordering a glass of chardonnay.

Alcohol niches are an important part of the new bar democracy, and I don't see this something-for-everyone perspective changing for a while. For instance, women, who control a lot of where this business goes, will continue to request low-calorie or "skinny" alcoholic beverages. These drinks have entered the mainstream, and as food and drink science continues to advance, so will lower-calorie spirits and cocktails. What we're seeing now in the market is just the beginning. Make sure a few of these "healthy" alternatives are part of your bar's repertoire, at least in the foreseeable future. Both men and women will seek out local, regional, and American-made spirits, beers, and wines. Local products are a great way to make your offerings "inclusive," while also giving patrons something they can't get at every other bar across the country.

Nightclubs and specialty venues will no longer be the exclusive home for live entertainment. Bands, singers, comedians, go-go dancers, and so on can and will add excitement and fun to almost any kind of bar. It's easy enough to find out what kind of following potential acts have by checking out their social media following.

Many bars, like other businesses, may find themselves in the position of having to find new revenue streams beyond what they have become accustomed to. This means being flexible and creative in terms of how your space can be used — and by whom. Multiconcept venues can increase revenue by offering up different themes using one kitchen and one bar. You can do a burger bar, a steak house, and a stir-fry offering all coming out of the same kitchen. Private event services can be offered during times when your regular nightclub or bar is "dark." Nightclubs might contract with a chef who can transform the club into a lunch venue during the day.

You can run two businesses from the same building if you think you can attract customers. The "after-dark" concept can become a robust revenue stream if your bar empties out after 10 P.M. Create a new logo with the name of your bar and the addition of "After Dark" and try serving more alcohol-oriented products. You could potentially add four more hours of revenue from a different set of customers by changing the tabletops and server costumes, adding candles, and turning up the music volume to create a truly different and authentic bar environment. If your location and community can support these sorts of ideas, why not give them a try?

Finally, give your best customers more of a say in what they want to see, taste, drink, and do in your bar to bring interactive democracy to the fore — after all, our great republic was hammered out in a tavern. Why shouldn't you carry on this tradition by welcoming customer suggestions — and acting on the good ones? What we say is opinion — what they say is fact.

# CONCLUSION

# Last Call

> I like bars just after they open for the evening. When the air inside is still cool and clean and everything is shiny . . . The first quiet drink of the evening in a quiet bar — that's wonderful.
>
> — RAYMOND CHANDLER, *THE LONG GOODBYE*

THE RULES HAVE CHANGED in every business. With each passing day, the likelihood that our markets and businesses will be "stimulated" back to the conditions we enjoyed in 2007 become less likely. Some pundits and economists called this economic climate a recession or a slow recovery from a depression. Other experts describe the transformation as a permanent or, at least, a very long-term "reset." I agree with the latter.

Consumer perceptions, preferences, and behavior have changed dramatically, and as a result complacency has been replaced with frequent reassessments of businesses, brands, products . . . and our establishments. Many of us have already seen customers modify their behavior, sometime significantly. Guest traffic, spending, and consumption have been affected at every level from fast food to five-star resorts. Whoever provides the greatest perceived value wins. Unfortunately, there will likely be far fewer restaurants and bars in business as a result of a marketplace that is still in the process of redefining and "resetting" itself.

Owners and managers who understand the reset will prosper; those who don't will be left behind. For those willing to adapt to a more cautious and demanding public, there is a robust opportunity to serve the human constant that survives all political cycles and social movements, and that is the desire for *social interaction.* Bars, pubs, taverns — call them whatever you want — are uniquely positioned to fulfill that desire and provide genuine value. Always have; always will. What revolutionary ideas of tomorrow will be sparked in bars today? How many barkeeps will inspire patrons to smile?

Speaking of which, making people smile is a nice legacy. The bar and restaurant business is a place where you can continue that legacy on a daily basis. It's one of the reasons why I love the bar business so much. I've based a lot of my strategies on that factor — what do I need to do to delight a customer and win his or her loyalty? It's the same question every business owner needs to ask. The answer will never be about price, even though spending habits have changed. No one leaves a great bar talking about the high prices. They only leave a lousy bar and talk about the prices. Raise your bar to match your prices; don't lower your prices to match your bar! Don't be cheaper — be better.

*Bar Rescue* has a pretty good track record demonstrating these principles — about 80 percent of the bars we've turned around have stayed the course. Not bad for less than a week's worth of work—and with bars that were really struggling. Unfortunately, not every bar I rescue succeeds in the end—owners revert to bad management and service habits, stubbornly cling to failed concepts, or have debt so crushing that nothing short of a miracle could change its downward trajectory.

You don't have to make these mistakes. The bar business is a growth industry and there are plenty of opportunities to make money and create the legacy of smiles *if* you do it right. Before, during, and after the recession that started in 2008, demand for all kinds of service people—including waitstaff, servers, cooks, and bartenders—*increased* dramatically. According to the Bureau of Labor Statistics, 545,000 jobs were added to the economy between 2010 and 2012 in "food services and drinking places." That is about 30 percent of the net increase in employment (1.84 million) during those two years. Demand for these workers will continue to expand. Good times and bad, bars never go out of style.

The information in this book has shown you how a great bar transcends economic conditions—if you're willing to put in the work required. The most enduring path to success in the bar business, or any other kind of business, is the one that empowers customers, respects them, and creates a perception of genuine value from experiences and transactions. You can never lose if you do these things. Are you ready to take the risk? It's a wild ride—but so worth it when done right. Remember, great transactions create fantastic reactions . . . and the best reactions create revenue. This industry has taken me to the Promised Land and I could not ask for more. Now it's your turn.

APPENDIX

# Create the Perfect Menu

You can control many customer reactions through the look and feel of your menu and its "content" (names of items, descriptions, and prices). Simply reformatting and simplifying a menu can increase sales. When I work with national, regional, or independent bar and restaurant owners, including those on *Bar Rescue,* we begin reengineering this way:

1. Identify the highest profit contributors for each menu category (appetizers, entrée groups, desserts, etc.) *in dollars,* not percentages — in other words, the items that make the most actual money. Also seriously reconsider those items that are rarely ordered or are very low profit. Is there a legitimate reason to keep them on the menu, or can they be eliminated and replaced with something that may be more popular and profitable?
2. Once you know how many items you have, select the proper-sized menu format (one panel, double-sided

panel, two panels, or three panels). Do not use oversized menus — bar menus should not be larger than a standard piece of paper. Remember that people are looking at the menu at a bar or a small table, not in a large dining room. Think scale. Make sure the font you use is very easy to read: simple and not too small. Stay away from elaborate script fonts. Remember, bars and many restaurants are dark, so design a menu that people sitting under dim lights can read. Keep the design straightforward by using three to four different fonts to differentiate section headings (appetizers, entrées, desserts, small plates, etc.). Color is fine as long as it does not interfere with readability. Menu print should be in high contrast against the background color.

3. Next, maximize your menu's sales potential by using all the sales-increasing design ideas I share below.

### *Food Menu Merchandising*

1. Boxing an item on a menu increases its sales up to 20 percent. Don't we want customers to order a bar's best, most well-known, popular, or profitable items? How do guests know which items these are? We box them.
2. A drop shadow on a menu item can increase the sales of that item up to 14 percent.
3. Designating special dishes with titles such as "Chef's Special" or "House Specialty" can increase the sales of that item by 12 percent.

4. Listing order matters. Every menu format has a visual sweet spot—the spot that gets the most attention by the human eye. Those sweet spots are where you want your most profitable boxes. Guests have a propensity to order the *top one* and *bottom two* items on single lists of appetizers, entrées, and desserts. These are excellent places to promote your most profitable and crowd-pleasing items.
5. Price points provide opportunity. For example, a food item priced at $5.50 has the same value perception as an item at $5.95 does. So you can pick up an extra 45¢ every time the item is sold with little or no negative guest reaction. Look at the math with two menu items. If you get a hundred orders for those two items each day, that's 90¢ a hundred times a day, seven days a week, for fifty-two weeks: $32,760. This is a lot of money. Conversely, increasing an item's price from $5.95 to $6.00 will likely cause a significant change in perceived value—for only a nickel! Too often menu pricing leaves money on the table.
6. Menu options make a huge impact upon your sales. Here are some quick ideas:

   * Entrée Add-Ons: If you sell steaks, implement a surf-and-turf upgrade. You can use preskewered shrimp and other easy items. If you sell a lot of fish, feature a few beef or chicken dishes.

   * Two-Sized Appetizers: We have had lots of success with two-sized appetizers. For example, rather than

just a six-piece shrimp cocktail, why not offer the "king cocktail" with eight pieces of shrimp too? About 30 percent of guests ordering the shrimp will order the larger one, and now you've increased your check by $3 to $4 a couple of hundred times a week.

* The Big Beef Motivation: If you sell steak, feature a really big one — a 24-ounce porterhouse or something similar. About 30 percent of male guests ordering steaks will order it, raising your check by $8 or more. This works with burgers too — you can offer a 5-, 8-, or 12-ounce burger and make $3 to $4 more on every large burger you sell.

* Small Desserts: I love to feature "the World's Smallest Hot Fudge Sundae" and I can sell the heck out of it. Guests who normally do not order dessert "get it" and say, "What's the harm? It's only a few bites." I can add $2.95 to a lot of checks because of this.

* Special, Unique Items: If Outback Steakhouse's Bloomin' Onion was instead a plate of familiar onion rings, would it sell as many? Of course not. Yet we take the simple approach all the time, especially in bar food programs, when a more original approach is no more costly or difficult to achieve, but much more profitable. Seek out new presentations for trusted standbys, and use your imagination (or your servers') to come up with fun names to create interest. Don't accept mediocrity. Make your program and items stand out.

## Beverage and Cocktail Merchandising

Like food sales, maximizing beverage sales per guest requires special merchandising techniques. The following strategies are very powerful. Often they can have a combined effect that increases beverage revenue per guest by more than 11 percent. Marketing drinks properly goes right back to understanding your market. Several years ago, I ran a bar on the East Coast and it did phenomenally well with "tooters" (test tube shots) called Blue Hawaii. These are very low-proof cocktails served in test tubes sold from specially made racks and they're really fun. There are generally thirty tubes to a rack. Servers walk around the room and sell tooters right from the rack for $2 or $3 each. The guest has to drink the cocktail quickly and put it back in the rack. I sold Blue Hawaiis night after night in that East Coast bar.

At the same time, I had taken over the Hollywood Palace in Los Angeles, and I put the Blue Hawaii program in that venue too. The servers could not make a dent in customers' interest in the drink—maybe we sold eleven. I thought, "What the heck is going on? I sell hundreds on the East Coast. What's wrong?" I talked to one of the bartenders. "Jon, this is Hollywood. We don't like cute. Everyone's dressed in black. Change the name to Blue Death and see what happens." Okay—I was game. We changed the name of the same drink and we sold nine hundred *that night.*

That is the power of branding and merchandising for your market. Sex on the Beach would not sell well if it had a different name because, let's face it, it's not the greatest-tasting cocktail. But people love ordering it. At sports bars, I would also put a drink or a food item "in honor of Moose Munson," and people would always order it and ask me about Moose. I'd say, "Oh, man, you don't know Moose Munson? Are you nuts? Look him up when you get home." There is no such sports person as Moose Munson. It was fun, and that's what sports bars are about. Here are a few other cocktail marketing ideas:

1. Cocktail Board: Hang a four-by-five-foot "martini" or "Special Beverages" board over your bar. Guests will respond to great names, interesting items, and special beverages that are prominently displayed (not table tents!).
2. Signature Drinks in Special Glassware: In nightclub environments, tooters work well — if you name them properly. So do shot glasses with "hooks" that hang on other glasses or beer bottles. But don't stop there. Drinks that are made important *become* important to the guest. Name your house drinks well; get them noticed. Names can be risqué, cute, or elegant, depending on your market.
3. Special Garnishes: Fresh or unusual garnishes and toppings like candied fruit slices, jellybeans, malted milk balls, gummy worms, espresso beans, fruits, citrus peel, coconut flakes, chocolate swirls, and marinated berries can go a long way to enticing guests. Have some fun. It does not have to be difficult.
4. Up-Selling by Size and Price:
   * Wine by the Glass: I like to feature a two-sized wine-by-the-glass program. With two-sized wineglasses, you can feature a standard 6-ounce and an 8- or 9-ounce wine pour. My research shows that approximately

22 percent of all guests who order wine by the glass will order the larger glass if they are told either on the menu or by the server that it is the "best value." This significantly increases wine-by-the-glass sales results. The concept is the same as 7-Eleven's Double Big Gulp (64 ounces). Who the hell can drink 64 ounces of Coke in one sitting? But people buy it because it seems like such a great deal. So if you instruct your servers to suggest that an 8- or 9-ounce glass is the "best value," you will sell more of that profitable size. Even wine bar sophisticates like a bargain. If you do *not* have the best value premise or designation either printed or spoken, a customer will usually order the smaller or cheaper glass.

* Draft Beer: Like wine, if you are not offering and selling a large glass of beer, you are missing an opportunity to make more money.

* Premium Soft Drinks: I hate pitchers of iced tea and I hate refillable soda . . . free refills, screw that. Give me premium soft drinks in bottles. In client restaurants, I often implement a display of popular bottled soft drinks, including SoBe, Snapple, Jones, diet-flavored colas, and a few name-brand still and bubbly waters. These beverages are appealing because they are unusual — most restaurants serve fountain sodas. Best of all, they command a far higher price than fountain and pitcher drinks — and there is no such thing as a free refill. Beautiful.

# INDEX